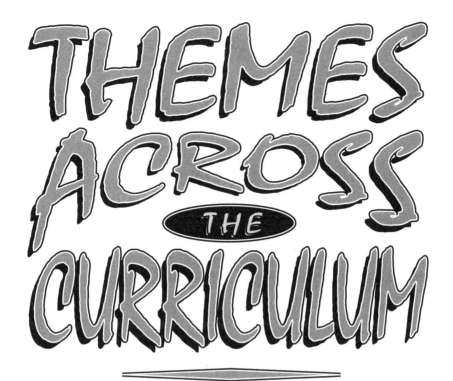

*Ready-to-Use
Activities & Projects
for the Elementary
Classroom*

KARL A. MATZ

**THE CENTER FOR APPLIED
RESEARCH IN EDUCATION**
West Nyack, New York 10994

Prentice-Hall International (UK) Limited, *London*
Prentice-Hall of Australia Pty. Limited, *Sydney*
Prentice-Hall Canada, Inc., *Toronto*
Prentice-Hall Hispanoamericana, S.A., *Mexico*
Prentice-Hall of India Private Limited, *New Delhi*
Prentice-Hall of Japan, Inc., *Tokyo*
Simon & Schuster Asia Pte. Ltd., *Singapore*
Editora Prentice-Hall do Brasil, Ltda., *Rio de Janeiro*

©1995 by
PRENTICE HALL, Inc.
Englewood Cliffs, NJ

All rights reserved. No part of this book may be reproduced in any form or by any means, without permission in writing from the publisher.

10 9 8 7 6 5 4 3 2 1

Library of Congress Cataloging-in-Publication Data

Matz, Karl A.
   Themes across the curriculum:ready-to-use activities & projects for the elementary classroom/Karl A. Matz.
      p.   cm.
   Includes bibliographical references.
   ISBN 0-87628-907-3:$27.95
   1. Language arts– –Correlation with content subjects.
2. Education, Elementary– –Activity programs. 3. Language experience approach in education. I. Title.
LB1576.M394   1995
372.6– –dc20
                                                                        94–42472
                                                                           CIP

ISBN 0-87628-907-3

PRENTICE HALL
Career and Personal Development
Englewood Cliffs, NJ 07632
Simon & Schuster, A Paramount Communications Company

Printed in the United States of America

About the Author

Karl A. Matz, Ed.D. is an assistant professor of Curriculum and Instruction at Mankato State University in Minnesota. He is a former elementary teacher and continues to work in schools to "keep in touch" with the lives of students and teachers. Karl is interested in finding ways to integrate the curriculum so that children have the opportunity to extend their knowledge and improve their language skills simultaneously in authentic and meaningful ways. His articles have appeared in *Teaching K-8, the Writing Teacher, Science and Children, The Reading Teacher, The Arithmetic Teacher* and *Contemporary Education.*

To my wife Kathy for being the answer when all others failed.

Acknowledgments

Special thanks to Linda Nielsen and Jill Potts and the children of North Intermediate School, St. Peter, Minnesota.

Also, special thanks to the University of Chicago graduate student who I met on the Internet for her help in translating the parent letter into Spanish.

Why Use Thematic Teaching?

The ideas associated with thematic teaching are hardly new. Creative and energetic teachers have always recognized the values inherent in the thematic approach or "integrated curriculum." Many teachers, for example, will set aside a week for integrating a circus theme throughout the curriculum. They know that when the circus comes to town, it is difficult to get children to think of anything else. Therefore, they wisely tap that strong interest as a series of "teachable moments" that permeate the curriculum while the children's excitement is at its zenith.

Other teachers offer a holiday theme while children are filled with the anticipation of the winter holidays. Still other teachers tap children's natural excitement about the coming of summer, and provide books, models, arts and writing activities that explore the season. The teacher may look forward to these annual themes with the same delight that the children have. This is certainly due in part to the fact that they know how effective thematic teaching can be.

Teachers know, for example, that children's strong interest in the theme translates into high motivation for learning and that most external rewards become unnecessary. Children naturally become more astute and dedicated when the reading material is related to something in which they have high interest or extensive background knowledge.

Teachers also know that the skills traditionally learned through drill and practice become more relevant when they are applied to real and meaningful tasks. Children learn the skills more completely and understand them on far deeper levels when they use those skills in authentic reading and writing. The children are already motivated to learn the skills through interest and need.

Finally, teachers are aware that children's knowledge of concepts and their knowledge of language are extended through meaningful exploration of a theme in reading and writing activities. For example, in a thematic approach to Bears, children learn to spell "koala," find out that koalas are not really bears, learn the characteristics of koalas, and discover how bears and koalas are alike and different. Guiding children to deeper and deeper levels of understanding are goals every teacher embraces.

Then why don't teachers use thematic teaching more often? Simply because thematic teaching requires a huge investment of time. Simply ***knowing*** about these important attributes of the thematic approach is one thing, but finding the time they need to plan and organize the theme, to create or locate activities and materials or to gather related books, songs and poetry is something else entirely.

That is the purpose behind this book: to provide teachers with materials, activities, and lists of resources that they can easily integrate into the language arts and the content areas, thus providing children with opportunities to learn skills and concepts in authentic and meaningful ways.

Why Use Thematic Teaching? vii

About the Resource

Themes Across the Curriculum provides teachers of elementary-grade children with materials and activities related to 12 themes commonly found in the curricula of the elementary grades. You may select all the resources related to a topic in a fully integrated approach, or you may opt to use them individually for enrichment, extra practice, or as regular seatwork.

Each theme provides some or all of the following:

- **An Interactive Bulletin Board.** An illustration of the bulletin board is provided along with any patterns that can easily be enlarged and colored.

- **Related Reading**. An annotated bibliography of appropriate, easily obtainable books, comprehension activities, and skill sheets are provided.

- **Poetry** for choral reading, the titles of the books in which they can be found, and activities related to reading, appreciating and writing poetry are included. In most themes, selected poems are provided.

- **Language Arts activities** appear in connection with both the poetry and reading activities.

- **Science.** These activities include demonstrations, experiments, hands-on projects, and/or practice pages.

- **Math activities and practice sheets** specific to the mathematics skills and concepts of the grades—such as counting, adding, subtracting and communicating through mathematics—are provided. There is also a **"do-it-yourself"** sheet. It is formatted for the theme, but left blank so that any math skill may be integrated with the particular theme. (See "Snowpeople Arithmetic" located in the Winter theme.)

- **Social Studies activities** include projects, puzzles, and geography activities.

- **Art.** Some of these projects are classics, others are more contemporary, still others are new and different; but all are appropriate for the topic and for the age of the children.

- **Miscellaneous** materials such as certificates, puzzles, skill sheets, and record-keeping materials related to the theme are included where appropriate.

The inclusion of many topics and the complete gamut of materials provides you with many options, allowing you to use themes you may not otherwise have been able to teach, and to tailor the theme to your own unique needs, the children's readiness, and the available time. Thus, you may choose to integrate fully, using the topic as a vehicle for learning in every facet of the school day, as some teachers do, or you may employ the topic only in those subject areas you choose, for example, continuing the spelling program normally in use while integrating the theme throughout the rest of the school day. Another teacher may use the theme as an opportunity to show children how spelling skills relate to real writing tasks and will "take a break" from the regular spelling program occasionally to integrate spelling with the other language arts and the content areas.

Themes Across the Curriculum is not intended to be a "blueprint" that must be followed to the letter. Instead, it is intended to be a "tool chest" that allows you to tailor the themes to whatever special circumstances exist or to use the individual activities and practice pages as you see fit.

Karl A. Matz, Ed.D.

Contents

Why Use Thematic Teaching? • vi
The *Awesome* Factor! • xx
How to Use Reading Records • xxii
How to Use the Writing Process • xxiii
Notes on Integrating Spelling • xxv
How to Start a Bookslingers' Club • xxvii

**1—Autumn
A Time of Changes** • 1

Autumn Change (*bulletin board idea*) • 2

Reading

    Bibliography • 3
    Autumn Books I've Read (*reproducible*) • 5
    When Autumn Comes (*reproducible*) • 6
    Word Bird's Fall Words (*reproducible*) • 7
    The Hedgehog Feast (*reproducible*) • 8

Language Arts

    An Autumn Story (*reproducible*) • 9
    Analogies (*reproducible*) • 10
    Long Words (*reproducible*) • 11

Science

    Chlorophyll (*a teacher-led activity*) • 12
    Variation within Species (*a teacher-led activity with reproducible*) • 13
    The Equinox (*a teacher-led activity*) • 15

Math

    What Are My Stats? (*reproducible*) • 17
    Sunrise and Sunset (*reproducible*) • 18
    November Elections (*reproducible*) • 19

Social Studies

    All Hallow's Evening (*a teacher-led activity*) • 20
    A Multicultural Harvest Festival (*a teacher-led activity*) • 22

Social Studies/Language Arts

    The Last of the Patuxet (*a play*) • 24

Art

    Apple People (*reproducible*) • 29

2—Winter
Br-r-r! • 30

Reading Is Cool (*bulletin board idea*) • 31

Reading

    Bibliography • 32
    Winter Books I've Read (*reproducible*) • 34
    Has Winter Come? (*reproducible*) • 35
    Kate's Snowman (*reproducible*) • 36
    The Big Snow (*reproducible*) • 37

Language Arts

    Winter Words (*reproducible*) • 38
    Winter Writing Warmup (*reproducible*) • 39
    White Is Winter (*poem*) • 40
    Winter Is a Waiting Time (*poem*) • 40
    What Will the Birdies Do Then, the Poor Things? (*poem*) • 41
    Other Poetry Resources • 42
    Puppet Show (*a teacher-led activity with reproducible*) • 43
    The Snowkids (*a puppet play*) • 45

Science

    An "Icy" Experiment (*a teacher-led activity with reproducible*) • 48
    A Cool Science Problem (*reproducible*) • 50

Math/Science

    The Winter Solstice (*a teacher-led activity*) • 51

Math

    Snowpeople Arithmetic (*reproducible*) • 53
    Story Problems (*reproducible*) • 54

Social Studies

    Using Winter Count (*a teacher-led activity with reproducibles*) • 55
    The Truth About Eskimos (*reproducible*) • 59
    Is Your State Blue or Green? (*reproducible*) • 60

Contents

Art
    Snowglobes (*a teacher-led activity*) • 61
    Better Snowflakes (*a teacher-led activity*) • 62

3—SPRING
JUMPING INTO SPRING • 65

A Real Pot of Gold! (*bulletin board idea*) • 66

Reading
    Bibliography • 67
    Springtime Books I've Read (*reproducible*) • 69
    The Boy Who Didn't Believe in Spring (*reproducible*) • 70
    Hi, Mr. Robin! (*reproducible*) • 71
    A Poetry Lesson (*a teacher-led activity*) • 72

Language Arts
    Spring Walks (*reproducible*) • 74
    Lots of Action Going On! (*reproducible*) • 75
    Going on a Picnic (*a teacher-led activity*) • 76

Science
    Hydroponics (*a teacher-led activity*) • 77
    How Are They Different? (*reproducible*) • 78
    A Seasonal Terrarium (*a teacher-led activity*) • 79

Math/Science
    The Spring Equinox (*a teacher-led activity*) • 80

Math
    Baseball Fun (*reproducible*) • 82
    Spring Subtraction (*reproducible*) • 83

Social Studies
    Where Did My Jacket Begin? (*a teacher-led activity with reproducible*) • 84
    Vacation Time Is Almost Here! (*reproducible*) • 86
    Welcome Spring (*reproducible*) • 87

Art
    Magazine Butterflies (*a teacher-led activity with reproducible*) • 88

4—SUMMER
THE END OF THE SCHOOL YEAR • 90

Dive into Summer Reading (*bulletin board idea*) • 91

Reading

    Bibliography • 92
    Summer Books I've Read (*reproducible*) • 94
    A Summer Day (*reproducible*) • 95
    The Sun's Asleep Behind the Hill (*reproducible*) • 96
    Basil Brush at the Beach (*reproducible*) • 97

Language Arts

    Compounds (*reproducible*) • 98
    What's the Question? (*reproducible*) • 99
    Fact or Opinion (*reproducible*) • 100

Science

    Leaf Cuttings (*a teacher-led activity*) • 101
    A Sundial (*a teacher-led activity*) • 102
    Lawn Science (*a teacher-led activity*) • 103
    Fill in the Thermometer (*reproducible*) • 104

Math

    A Summer Friend (*reproducible*) • 105
    Ice Cream—Yummy! (*reproducible*) • 106

Social Studies

    Vacation Travel Guides (*a teacher-led activity with reproducible*) • 107
    Summer on Cleo's Island (*reproducible*) • 110

Art

    Let's Fly a Kite (*a teacher-led activity*) • 111

5—THE FAMILY
A THEME FOR ALL SEASONS • 114

We Are Family (*bulletin board idea*) • 115

Reading

    Bibliography • 116
    Books I've Read About Families (*reproducible*) • 120
    The Wednesday Surprise (*reproducible*) • 121
    All Kinds of Families (*reproducible*) • 122
    Yonder (*reproducible*) • 123

Contents **xiii**

Language Arts
    Describe the Relationships *(reproducible)* • 124
    Family Facts *(reproducible)* • 125
    A Writing Activity *(reproducible)* • 126

Science
    Your Heredity *(reproducible)* • 127
    Animals as Parents *(reproducible)* • 128

Math
    The Alvarez Family *(reproducible)* • 129
    The Alvarez Family's Grocery Bill *(reproducible)* • 130
    The Alvarez Family Budget *(reproducible)* • 131

Social Studies
    My Relative's Biography *(reproducible)* • 132
    Tiyospaye *(a teacher-led activity with reproducibles)* • 133

Art
    A Personal Coat of Arms *(a teacher-led activity)* • 138

6—Circus
Boys and Girls of All Ages • 141

Come to the Circus *(bulletin board idea)* • 142

Reading
    Bibliography • 143
    Circus Books I've Read *(reproducible)* • 145
    Lenny and Lola *(two reproducibles)* • 146
    The Toy Circus *(reproducible)* • 148

Reading/Language Arts
    Clooney the Clown *(reproducible)* • 149
    Come to the Circus! *(poem)* • 150

Language Arts
    Circus Words *(reproducible)* • 151
    Fill in the Words *(reproducible)* • 152
    Follow the Directions *(reproducible)* • 153

Language Arts/Math
    Clown-a-Rounds *(a teacher-led activity with reproducible)* • 154

Science
    Caring for Your Own Elephant! *(reproducible)* • 156

Armand, the Acrobat (*a teacher-led activity with reproducible*) • 157

Math

Shapes (*reproducible*) • 159
The Juggling Clown (*reproducible*) • 160
The Circus Elephant (*reproducible*) • 161
What's the Sum? (*reproducible*) • 162
The Clown's Balloons (*reproducible*) • 163

Social Studies

Jobs in the Circus (*reproducible*) • 164
Traveling with the Circus (*reproducible*) • 165
Citizenship (*reproducible*) • 166

Art

Let's Make a Poster (*reproducible*) • 167
Laffy the Clown (*reproducible*) • 168

7—BEARS
A THEME YOU CAN REALLY SINK YOUR TEETH INTO • 169

Bear Stories (bulletin board idea) • 170

Reading

Bibliography • 171
Bear Books I Have Read (*reproducible*) • 174
Lost (*reproducible*) • 175
Little Bear (*two reproducibles*) • 176
Bread and Honey (*reproducible*) • 178
Corduroy (*reproducible*) • 179

Language Arts

Do You Know This Bear? (*poem*) • 180
Noun-Sense (*reproducible*) • 181
Play on Words (*reproducible*) • 182
Nouns About Bears (*reproducible*) • 183

Science

Bear Facts (*a teacher-led activity with reproducible*) • 184
Food for Bears (*reproducible*) • 186

Math

Counting and Sorting Bears (*a teacher-led activity with reproducibles*) • 187
The Bears' Arithmetic (*reproducible*) • 190
Measure Your Bear (*reproducible*) • 191

Contents

Social Studies/Language Arts/Science
  Brown Bear, Brown Bear, What Do You See? (*a teacher-led activity*) • 192

Social Studies
  Pandas and Koalas (*reproducible*) • 193
  Where Does This Bear Live? (*reproducible*) • 194

Art
  Make a Bear (*a teacher-led activity with reproducibles*) • 195
  Bear Necklaces (*a teacher-led activity*) • 197

8—FARMS
A CROP OF "TASTY" ACTIVITIES • 199

A Crop of Great Reading (*bulletin board idea*) • 200

Reading
  Bibliography • 201
  Books I've Read About Farms (*reproducible*) • 203
  The Auction (*reproducible*) • 204
  Tibber (*reproducible*) • 205
  Time to Go (*reproducible*) • 206

Reading/Language Arts
  Drylongso (*reproducible*) • 207

Language Arts
  A Letter for Aunt Minnie (*reproducible*) • 208
  Vocabulary (*reproducible*) • 209
  What Shall We Do on the Farm Today? (*poem*) • 210
  Mrs. Cornbloom's Farm (*flannel board story with patterns*) • 211

Science
  A Recipe for Beef Stew (*reproducible*) • 213
  An Integrated Activity for Oatmeal Pancakes (*a teacher-led activity*) • 214
  Eating the Growing Things (*reproducible*) • 216

Math
  Farmer O'Grady (*reproducible*) • 217
  The Clever Farmer (*a teacher-led activity with reproducible*) • 218

Social Studies
  From a Farm to Your Home (*two reproducibles*) • 220
  Scavenger Hunt (*reproducible*) • 222

Art
  What Is It? (*reproducible*) • 223

9—HABITAT
WE ALL NEED EACH OTHER • 225

This Is the Place to Be (bulletin board idea) • 226

Reading

    Bibliography • 228
    Books I've Read About Habitats (*reproducible*) • 231
    I Was Born in a Tree and Raised by Bees (*reproducible*) • 232
    Come to the Meadow (*reproducible*) • 233
    The Gift of the Tree (*reproducible*) • 234

Language Arts

    The Greb-Greb Fish (*poem*) • 235
    Five Ways to Respond to "The Greb-Greb Fish" (*a teacher-led activity*) • 236

Science

    Drought Comes to the Habitat (*a teacher-led activity with reproducible*) • 237
    Living and Nonliving Things (*reproducible*) • 239
    Beaks and Bills (*reproducible*) • 240

Math/Science/Language Arts

    A Habitat Game (*a teacher-led activity*) • 241

Math

    The Swineburn Swamp Party (*reproducible*) • 243
    Can You Help? (*reproducible*) • 244
    What's the Answer? (*reproducible*) • 245

Social Studies

    Endangered Animals (*reproducible*) • 246
    Habitat Temperatures (*reproducible*) • 247
    Where in the World? (*reproducible*) • 248

Art

    Interpreting Reality (*a teacher-led activity*) • 249

10—UNDERSEA
DIVING INTO THE WATERS • 251

So Much to See Under the Sea (bulletin board idea) • 252

Reading

    Bibliography • 253
    Books I've Read About Oceans and Seas (*reproducible*) • 255

Contents

    The Fisherman Under the Sea (*reproducible*) • 256
    The Cat Who Loved the Sea (*reproducible*) • 257
    Fish Is Fish (*reproducible*) • 258

Language Arts

    An Undersea Wordsearch (*reproducible*) • 259
    What's the Story? (*reproducible*) • 260
    Find the Adjectives (*reproducible*) • 261

Science

    Sink or Float? (*reproducible*) • 262
    Fishy Things (*a teacher-led activity with reproducible*) • 263
    Growing Brine Shrimp (*a teacher-led activity*) • 266

Math

    Undersea Pictures (*reproducible*) • 268
    Submerged Subtraction (*reproducible*) • 269
    Solve the Problems (*reproducible*) • 270
    Help the Pirate (*reproducible*) • 271

Social Studies

    Let's Read the Map (*reproducible*) • 272
    Which State? (*reproducible*) • 273

Art

    A "Fishy" Scene (*a teacher-led activity with pattern*) • 274

11—Ecology
Stop the Destruction • 277

Our Pollution Solution (*bulletin board idea*) • 279

Reading

    Bibliography • 280
    Ecology Books I've Read (*reproducible*) • 282
    The Paper Bag Prince (*reproducible*) • 283
    The Great Kapok Tree (*reproducible*) • 284
    The Salamander Room (*reproducible*) • 285

Language Arts

    Poetry from Trash! (*a teacher-led activity*) • 286
    State Your Case (*reproducible*) • 287
    What I Think About Ecology (*reproducible*) • 288
    We Care About the Earth (*a teacher-led activity*) • 289

Science

    The Balance of Nature (*reproducible*) • 290
    Animals in the Wild (*reproducible*) • 292
    Organic Material (*a teacher-led activity with reproducibles*) • 293

Math

    Math Problems to Solve (*reproducible*) • 296
    Complete the Multiplication Table (*reproducible*) • 297

Social Studies

    Light the Bulbs (*reproducible*) • 298
    Climb the Kapok Tree (*reproducible*) • 299
    Which Package Is Better? (*reproducible*) • 300

Art

    Recycle Those Egg Cartons (*reproducible*) • 301

12—GLOBAL CARNIVAL
SHARING, SPEAKING, LISTENING • 303

Celebrate the World (*bulletin board idea*) • 304

Reading

    Bibliography • 305
    Global Books I've Read (*reproducible*) • 307
    Teammates (*reproducible*) • 308
    Mississippi Bridge (*three reproducibles*) • 309

Language Arts

    Colors (*reproducible*) • 312
    A Poem for Two Voices (*a teacher-led activity with reproducible*) • 313
    Maybe I'll Just Stay Me! (*poem for choral reading*) • 316
    If Only You'd Try (*poem with reproducible*) • 317
    The Wise Milkmaid (*a play with teacher-led activities and reproducible*) • 319
    Write a Folktale! (*reproducible*) • 326

Science

    Preserving Food (*a teacher-led activity*) • 327
    Water Purification (*a teacher-led activity*) • 329

Math

    Measure Me! (*reproducible*) • 331
    Solve the Problems (*reproducible*) • 332
    What's the Message? (*reproducible*) • 333

Social Studies

    In Which Direction? (*reproducible*) • 334
    In Which Environment? (*reproducible*) • 335
    Where Should You Be? (*reproducible*) • 336

Art

    Ojo de Dios, Spanish for Eye of God (*a teacher-led activity*) • 337

The AWESOME Factor!

The **AWESOME Factor Chart** is a response to a book or story that the children have read or have had read to them. Children, in groups of four to six, choose a category (for example, excitement, sadness, humor), record the significant events in the story related to that category, and "graph" them. The graphing is very subjective and is based on group decisions rather than any real objective data, but it does allow children the opportunity to compare and contrast the relationships between and among story events. The activity also encourages discussion, provides children with an opportunity to synthesize and prioritize events in a story, and to comprehend on a deep level. In addition, it provides a context in which to discuss story climaxes and thus the structure of stories.

Here is a chart of *The Three Pigs* as an example.

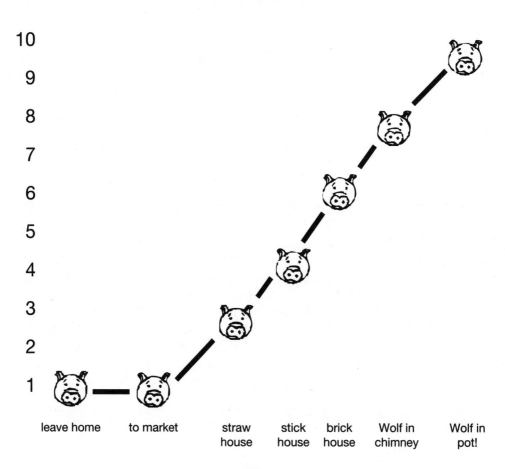

Procedure

1. Before a story is read to the class, organize the children into groups of 4 to 6. Explain that certain events in a story are more exciting, for some reason, than other events.

2. Invite the children to identify the important events in *The Three Pigs*.

3. Ask the children to identify the excitement levels of these events. Each event should be compared to the one before it to determine a reasonable level. For example, the tension when the wolf blows down the stick house is higher than the tension that existed when the wolf blew down the straw house.

4. Direct the groups to identify and record the important events as you read to them. If it is a book that will be shared over several days, time should be allotted to let the groups discuss and choose the events from the day's reading.

5. When the reading is done, children can select an element of the story to graph. Mildred Taylor's *Mississippi Bridge* usually inspires graphs of The Prejudice Factor, The Thrill Factor, The Danger Factor, and others.

6. The groups should condense their list of events to the 10 or 12 they consider to be most important.

7. Graphs should be creative, colorful, and suitable for display.

8. The activity can be used with any story. The children's work will become increasingly sophisticated and creative as they gain more experience with the activity.

How to Use Reading Records

Each theme includes a page entitled "Books I've Read About…" or a similar title. This page has five lines on which children can list up to five books they've read by title and author. The page can serve as motivation, record keeping, and to provide children with opportunities to be involved in the evaluation of their work. Following are several suggestions for using these reading records.

1. The page can be used as a recording device that is placed in the child's portfolio at the end of each unit. They can be shared with parents at various times during the year.

2. The page can be used as a reinforcer/motivator for readers who struggle or are reluctant. Five books can be an attainable goal for most children if the time frame and text difficulty are adapted to the child's needs and abilities.

3. The page can be used to make "a chain" down the wall or along one wall in the hallway to demonstrate and advertise the kinds and numbers of books the class, as a whole, has read.

4. The page can be used to encourage/monitor children's independent reading of books from the bibliography. A bulletin board or wall space can be set aside to post the page as an accomplishment. Let children maintain the record themselves, then color it and mount it on construction paper for display.

How to Use the Writing Process

1. ***Brainstorm.*** Make sure the children have read one or more of the books in the bibliography for the theme. Engage the children in active brainstorming in response to a question such as "What kinds of things do we see and hear in a forest?" or "What are some things you like about your friend?" Write the ideas they offer on the chalkboard, easel paper, or the overhead where they are easily seen and accessible.

2. ***First draft.*** Invite children to write a story, such as "The Time I Ran Away" or "My Visit to a Farm," using vocabulary and concepts from the theme. The story can be either personal narrative or fiction. The thematic spelling list and the brainstorming activity will provide most of the high-frequency words, so this should reduce the number of requests for correct spellings. In any case, the first draft need not be perfect. Corrections can be made later in the Editing stage, after the child's thoughts and ideas have been written down.

3. ***When "writer's block" occurs.*** Most of the concepts in these themes are familiar enough that no one should complain "I can't think of anything!" Should that happen, it will usually be enough to seat that child with another child who is actively writing. Good ideas are contagious. But if necessary provide a "story starter" and encourage the child to write on that topic using words from the spelling list and the brainstorming.

4. ***Peer conference.*** First drafts can be shared with peers to aid in revision. Children will need to learn how to support and help one another, not merely to criticize or praise. These techniques can also be learned in large group sharing where you can facilitate appropriate responses. One useful strategy is to invite children in groups of four to share first drafts. After one of the authors reads, each listener in turn can offer a word of praise, a question, and a suggestion. For example:

   > I really like the part where you talk about how the horse scared you. What made you feel afraid? Maybe you could say, "It seemed so big I was afraid it might step on me!"

5. ***Edit writing errors.*** When stories have been revised, any necessary editing can be done. It is best to be flexible with younger children's writing so as not to discourage them; but constantly model and state the importance of correct spelling and legible handwriting.

6. ***Publish.*** To a writer, one of the most important reasons to write is sharing the work with others. One method of "publishing" is THE AUTHOR'S CHAIR. This is simply a chair set up in front of the group, with an ornate sign above it. The writer sits in the chair and shares the story he or she wrote. You or the writer can then choose three or four volunteers who offer "praise words"—something they liked about the story. This is not a time for suggestions of revision—these are finished works and should be in their final form.

Some Additional Notes

If thematic teaching is used periodically throughout the year, the writing from each thematic topic area can be gathered into a book and preserved in the classroom library. Don't worry if these are only rarely read, because an equally important aspect of publishing is simply to honor the works and the authors.

Story starters should be used sparingly. One purpose of the writing process is to teach children to express themselves in writing and to take ownership of the work. Story starters can be a temporary solution to writer's block, but in the end the children must find their own voices.

Notes on Integrating Spelling

When the content areas and the language arts are integrated, spelling becomes an especially important issue. Children are reading and writing about topics and concepts that are of interest to them. They find, however, that each theme has certain specialized vocabulary they may need and want to use. It makes sense that the words they study and learn to spell for their weekly spelling test are words they will find useful in their reading and writing.

How to Go About It

A spelling unit for thematic teaching can be accomplished with a fairly simple and easily adapted process.

1. **Brainstorm:** Invite the children to think of words relating to the theme and offer them at will. Write these on chart paper, the chalkboard, or an overhead as they are offered. Get as many as the children can think of.

2. **Prioritize the List:** Identify the 15 or 20 words that are most important or most useful from the list. The students may enjoy doing this, and you can encourage critical thinking by asking them to explain why certain words are more important than others.

3. **Practice the List:** The words can be practiced in several realistic and authentic ways.

    a. *Invite children to alphabetize the list.* They become very proficient at this in a relatively short time. The skill is useful for dictionaries, card catalogs, encyclopedae, thesauri, and other forms of reference material.

    b. *Write a cumulative story using the words.* A child writes a sentence using one of the words and calls on another child to write a second, but related sentence using another of the words—and so on—until the words are all used. You may wish to choose the "scribes" rather than have children make the choices, or organize the class into groups of 6 to 9 and each child contributes a sentence. The result should be a cohesive story.

    c. *Look-Cover-Write-Check.* Research tells us that this is still the best way to study words. With the list in hand, the child looks at a word, covers it, then writes it from memory. If, after checking, the word is not correctly spelled, the child covers and writes again. If the word is correct, the child goes on to the next word and continues until all words are correctly spelled. This practice can be done anytime and should be done twice or three times before the test.

d. *Have a Contest.* Invite children to write the sentences for the spelling test. Post them and have a silent election in which children vote for the sentences they like the best. The winning sentences become a part of the Friday spelling test.

A Recommended Weekly Procedure

Monday: Brainstorm and prioritize the list.

Tuesday: Alphabetize the list (cooperative or individually).

Wednesday: Practice test

Thursday: Individual and team practice (activities **b-d** above)

Friday: Final test.

SAMPLE Theme: Under sea

Monday: *Brainstorm:* (tide, waves, beach, seaweed, whale, dolphin, fish, starfish, sharks, clam, crabs, lobster, surf, island, scuba, jellyfish, boat, net, ship, sand, seashells, turtles, submarine, salt, sailor)

Prioritized list (tide, sand, salt, waves, surf, whale, shark, dolphin, island, beach, seaweed, seashells, crab, starfish, net)

Tuesday: *In pairs to alphabetize:* (beach, crab, dolphin, island, net, salt, sand, seashells, seaweed, shark, starfish, surf, tide, waves, whale)

Wednesday: *Practice test*

Thursday: *Spelling sentence contest and/or in pairs to Look-Cover-Write-Check*

Friday: *Final test*

How to Start
A Bookslingers' Club

1. The BOOKSLINGERS' CLUB is a motivational program in the guise of an "elite club." It is not really elite, since any child in the class who chooses to can become a member by sharing a predetermined number of books at the regularly scheduled BOOKSLINGERS' CLUB meetings. There are three levels of membership: Bronze, Silver, and Gold.

2. The children achieve each level by sharing a predetermined number of books. Perhaps you will decide that each time a child shares one book at a club meeting, that child advances a level. Perhaps you will want the child to share three books (once each meeting) to earn the next level. Whatever seems appropriate is fine.

3. The class chooses a president to preside over the meetings of the club. The president can be selected by normal democratic process or by drawing. You and/or the class may decide how long the president will serve. Perhaps a new president will be chosen for each bi-weekly meeting, or perhaps a new president will be selected each month. Any procedure will work.

4. Silver and Gold levels seem to become more precious if a perk is attached to them. For example:

    a. The class may decide that only gold members can serve as president.

    b. You may choose to line up students for lunch twice a month according to their Bookslingers' Club rank.

    c. The class may have a special bulletin board that features the name and/or photo (see #7 below) of all those who have achieved the rank of Bookslinger Gold Class. The circumstances of the classroom or the school will provide other ideas. It is most important that children know that no one is excluded from these perks and that anyone can achieve them if they choose to.

5. During the time period in which a theme is being celebrated, the class will hold a meeting of the BOOKSLINGERS' CLUB. During this meeting certain students who have signed up to do so, will give a "sales pitch" for a book related to the theme which that child has read.

6. You can prepare the following for the president to read at the start of each BOOKSLINGERS' CLUB meeting:

> Welcome to this meeting of the Bookslingers Club. Today we will hear about several books that have a Winter theme. Wendy Mullins will be going for the gold . . .

7. Each student who has signed up to share a book is introduced by the president. If the child has met the requirement, that child is awarded a certificate indicating the level and signed by you and/or the club president. (Sample certificates are given at the end of this section.) It's nice to formalize this by photographing the child shaking the president's hand, as is done in the local newspaper. This adds prestige to the achievement, and to the presidency.

8. The photographs can be displayed on a bulletin board set aside especially for that purpose.

9. The president then closes the meeting by saying:

> Congratulations to all of today's bookslingers. Our next meeting will feature books with a Habitat theme. I hope many of you will sign up to read one.

10. During subsequent themes, children who wish to do so may sign up in advance to present books related to the new theme. It is advisable to limit the number who can sign up. This adds not only prestige—by making Gold Class harder to achieve—it also simplifies the scheduling of meetings.

Autumn
A Time of Changes

Autumn is a time of change. The seasons change from the lazy days of summer to the barren gray days of late fall. There are new teachers and classmates and a whole set of new things to learn. There are also elections that bring new politicians. There are holidays with historical roots and cultural origins. It's a rich time for learning.

The only problem is deciding *when* to plan an integrated theme about Autumn. It really doesn't begin until the third week of school and it lasts until late December. The changing leaves that are classic images of autumn really peak sometime between late September to mid October. Halloween is in late October, Election Day is in early November, Thanksgiving is three weeks later, and the Winter Solstice is not until December 21.

When does a teacher "do" an Autumn theme?

One recommendation is to prepare for the celebration by completing the Equinox activity on September 23. Save that (you'll do similar activities December 21, March 21, and early June), then plan to begin the Autumn theme beginning with Halloween. Whether you celebrate this day or not, there is an interesting historical origin to the traditions. That is also the time to teach a civics lesson by watching local elections and taking part in the debates over issues. Have children bring newspaper stories, tape the local news, and obtain campaign literature. Have debates in a "classroom caucus" and hold a mock election. Also, the scientific changes of Autumn should be well underway. Begin preparing the play "Last of the Patuxet," a Social Studies activity that reveals some important and little-known facts about Squanto. You'll want to perform this play sometime around Thanksgiving. A high-tech approach is to videotape the performance at your convenience and share it with other classrooms to view at their convenience. You also have the advantage of production techniques: turning off the camera during scene changes, close-ups on people who are speaking, varieties of camera angles to keep the viewer involved, and lighting techniques like silhouettes.

A study of Autumn is really necessary, but as with all the themes, this one is designed to provide opportunities and choice. Use the resources in whatever order and in whatever way seems most appropriate to the age of the children you teach.

Bulletin Board Idea

# Bibliography

Allington, R. *Autumn*. Milwaukee: Raintree, 1981 **(32 pages)**. Excellent for a beginning discussion of the season and activities normally associated with it.

Dillon, J. *Jeb Scarecrow's Pumpkin Patch*. Boston: Houghton-Mifflin, 1992 **(32 pages)**. Jeb comes up with a wonderful plan to scare the crows away from his pumpkin patch.

Fox, C. *When Autumn Comes*. Chicago: Reilley & Lee, 1966 **(unpaged)**. A picture book with easy-to-read text that explores the beauty of autumn. (Two books with this title appear in this bibliography.)

Jones, J. *Projects for Autumn*. Ada, OK: Garrett Educational, 1989 **(31 pages)**. An integration treasure, with games, activities, arts, crafts, and recipes for Autumn!

Heuck, S. *Who Stole the Apples?* New York: Alfred Knopf, 1986 **(28 pages)**. A horse and a bear are hot on the trail of some thief who stole apples from a tree in the forest clearing.

Holden, E. *The Hedgehog Feast*. New York: EP Dutton, 1978 **(20 pages)**. The hedgehog holds a lavish harvest feast in celebration of the coming hibernation. Beautiful watercolor art.

Maass, R. *When Autumn Comes*. New York: Holt, 1990 **(32 pages)**. Beautiful color photos and well-written text reveal the changes present in the coming of autumn. (Two different books with this title appear in this bibliography.)

Mahy, M. *Leaf Magic*. New York: Parents' Magazine Press, 1976 **(29 pages)**. Running would be more fun with a dog, but all Michael gets on an autumn day is an orange leaf that follows him everywhere he goes.

Markle, S. *Exploring Autumn: A Season of Science Activities, Puzzlers and Games*. New York: Atheneum, 1991 **(152 pages)**. A good resource for the teacher. Rich with activities and experiments to teach and impress the concepts of changing seasons and the characteristics of autumn specifically.

McDonald, M. *The Great Pumpkin Switch*. New York: Orchard Books, 1992 **(32 pages)**. Grandpa reveals a secret from his childhood of how he and his friend smashed great-auntie's pumpkin and had to find another to replace it.

Moncure, J. *Word Bird's Fall Words*. Elgin, IL: Child's World. 1985 **(32 pages)**. One of Jane Moncure's four seasons Word Bird books. In this easy reader, Word Bird gathers words for fall and puts them in his word house.

Rockwell, A. *Apples and Pumpkins*. New York: Macmillan, 1989 (24 pages). A family visits Farmer Comstock to pick apples and pumpkins in preparation for Halloween night.

Rosen, M. *Autumn Festivals*. New York: Bookwright, 1990 (32 pages). Autumn and harvest celebrations and holidays from around the world.

Roth, H. *Autumn Days*. New York: Grossett & Dunlap, 1986 (12 pages). Easy reader that explores the activities of the season: rolling in leaves, picking apples, and searching for a Halloween pumpkin.

Rowley, A. *A Sunday in Autumn*. Syracuse, NY: LW Singer Co., 1967 (31 pages). The changing colors of leaves, the migrating birds, and other signs of the coming autumn.

Santrey, L. *Autumn*. Mahwah, NJ: Troll Associates, 1983 (32 pages). Beautiful color photography teaches children how plants and animals prepare during autumn for the coming winter.

Schweninger, A. *Autumn Days*. New York: Viking, 1991 (32 pages). A scientific look at the changes of autumn in a way that children will understand and enjoy.

Silverman, E. *Big Pumpkin*. New York: Macmillan, 1992 (unpaged). A Halloween story about a witch who is trying to remove a huge pumpkin. She finds she is unable to do so without help. But who will help her?

Skofield, J. *Nightdances*. New York: Harper & Row, 1986 (32 pages). A family dances in the dark of an autumn night before settling down to sleep.

Thomson, R. *Autumn*. New York: Franklin Watts, 1989 (32 pages). The third book in this bibliography with this title, but this one is a book of autumn arts and crafts. Very handy for integrating the concepts through arts.

Tresselt, A. *Autumn Harvest*. New York: Lothrop, Lee & Shepard, 1951 (unpaged). A charming story that takes the reader through the autumn harvest. One can almost feel the crisp air and hear the migrating geese.

Warren, J. *Scissor Stories for Fall*. Everett, WA: Totline Press, 1984 (80 pages). One of many books in the cut-and-tell series. Unusual, unique and charming, with active reading ideas.

Zapler, G. *Science in Summer and Fall*. Garden City, NY: Doubleday, 1974 (177 pages). Another resource for the teacher. Offers activities and experiments that teach about the changes that occur as summer gives way to fall.

NAME_____

AUTUMN BOOKS I'VE READ

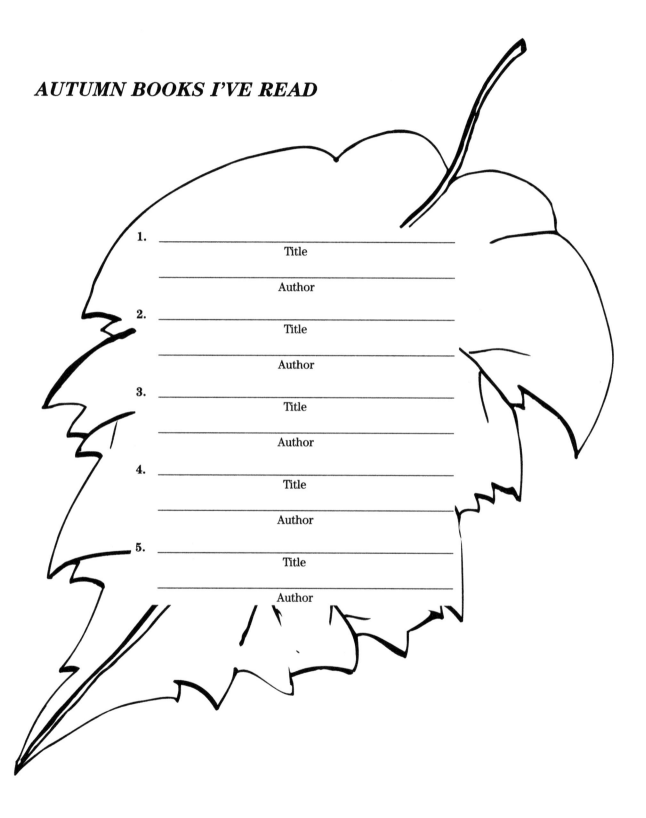

1. _____
   Title
   _____
   Author
2. _____
   Title
   _____
   Author
3. _____
   Title
   _____
   Author
4. _____
   Title
   _____
   Author
5. _____
   Title
   _____
   Author

© 1995 by The Center for Applied Research in Education

When Autumn Comes
by
Robert Maass

NAME _____

Directions:
This book tells of many changes that happen during autumn. Think of something that plants, animals, the weather, or people do during autumn. Write your idea on the lines below. Use a complete sentence, then draw a picture. Your page will be part of a class book.

Word Bird's Fall Words
by
Jane Moncure

NAME _____

Directions:

Nouns are names for people, places, and things. Be like Word Bird and list all the nouns you might find in a forest on an autumn day.

The Hedgehog Feast
by
Edith Holden

NAME _____

1. If you were going to invite your friends to come to a harvest feast like hedgehog, what foods would you serve? _____
   _____

2. People have feasts to celebrate many different things. List three.

   _____

   _____

   _____

3. Look at your list above. Have you been to a feast for one of these reasons? Write about it. Why was the feast held? Who was there? What foods were served? Use complete sentences, and continue on the back of the sheet if necessary.

   _____
   _____
   _____
   _____
   _____
   _____
   _____
   _____
   _____
   _____

NAME _____

An Autumn Story

Directions:

Think up words for each clue. Then use them to complete the autumn story below.

1. _____ 2. _____
   weather word   animal

3. _____ 4. _____
   plant   illness

5. _____ 6. _____
   another animal   hobby

7. _____ 8. _____
   clothing   superlative adjective

9. _____ 10. _____
   adjective   common noun

It was a 1. _____ autumn morning. Benny the 2. _____ had gathered the last of his 3. _____ and hid it in his home. He had just a bit of 4. _____, so he was anxious to begin his long winter nap. Just as he was lying down there was a knock at the door. It was Arnold the 5. _____. He wanted to know if Benny would help him with his 6. _____. Benny was about to answer when he noticed that Arnold was wearing a 7. _____ on his head.

"That's the 8. _____ thing I ever saw," said Benny.

"Well," said Arnold. "You're not so 9. _____ yourself."

Arnold left angrily and Benny went right to sleep and began dreaming about _____.

9 Language Arts

Analogies

Directions:

Analogies are ways of comparing two things. Here's an example:

> **Hand** is to **mitten** as **foot** is to _____.

You might have said "sock," "shoe," or "boot." Try these:

1. **Trees** are to **leaves** as **heads** are to _____.

2. **June** is to **summer** as **October** is to _____.

3. **Bear** is to **cave** as **bird** is to _____.

4. **Cereal** is to **corn** as **ice cream** is to _____.

5. **President** is to **Lincoln** as **teacher** is to _____.

6. **Pumpkin** is to **Peter** as **apple** is to _____.

7. **Picnic** is to **July 4th** as **turkey** is to _____.

8. **Summer** is to **swimsuit** as **autumn** is to _____.

9. **Spring** is to **School's Out** as **autumn** is to _____.

10. **Hibernate** is to **bears** as **migrate** is to _____.

Language Arts

NAME _____

Long Words

Directions:

Use the clue to help you think of a long word. How many syllables can you get all together? Compare with your friends.

WORD	Syllables
A kind of tree _____	_____
A kind of animal _____	_____
A northern state _____	_____
A town or city in that state _____	_____
A state capital _____	_____
A politician _____	_____
Something about Christopher Columbus _____	_____
Something about the Pilgrims _____	_____
Total number of syllables	_____

Chlorophyll
(a teacher-led activity)

Purpose:

Most people (not just children) are unaware of the reason why leaves change color. This experiment will make it clear by allowing children to remove chlorophyll from a leaf.

Materials:

One leaf per student or group
Boiling water
One small cup of rubbing alcohol per student or group
One small bowl of very warm water per student or group

Procedure:

1. Soak the leaves in boiling water for 10-15 minutes.
2. Have groups of students place a leaf, fresh from the boiling water, in the cup with just rubbing alcohol to cover the leaf. Let this cup sit in a bowl of very warm water for one hour. Change the water every 15 minutes to keep it warm.
3. The leaf will very soon begin to lose its chlorophyll. If maintained long enough, the leaf will become a dull white color.
4. Explain to the children that this chlorophyll is the substance that allows the plant to make food from sunlight, water, and soil nutrients. When the green is gone, the other colors become visible. Share this poem:

I asked the trees so green and tall

Why they change colors in the Fall.

The color is always there they say

But the chlorophyll has gone away.

Variation within Species
(a teacher-led activity)

Purpose:

All living things have variety within the species. This is part of nature.

Materials:

Per Group

About 100 leaves from the same tree (each group can have leaves from a different tree)

"Different Ways to Be" worksheet

Procedure:

1. Arrange children into groups of four.
2. *Brainstorm*: Are there variations among people? What variations can we expect to see in leaves?
3. Pass out the leaves and tell groups to arrange them according to some characteristic (such as size, amount of one color, or general shape).
4. Ask the groups to find the ten "best" leaves. (Let the children decide what that means.)
5. *Have each group report*: What characteristic makes them "best"? Who decides this? What criteria do we use to determine quality of leaves, people, or animals?
6. *Extend the learning*: Provide children with the "Different Ways to Be" activity sheet.

Different Ways to Be

Directions:

After arranging the leaves, answer the questions on the lines below.

1. What variation did your group use to arrange the leaves?
   _____

2. What are some other variations you might have used?
   _____
   _____

3. Think about an animal such as a bird or cat. What are some ways that a group of the same animal can differ?
   _____
   _____

4. What are some ways that people differ? List as many as you can.

   _____
   _____
   _____
   _____
   _____
   _____
   _____
   _____

Autumn

The Equinox
(a teacher-led activity)

Concept:

Observe the astronomical changes of autumn.

You need:

Metersticks
A sunny day
The weather report from today's newspaper

Procedure:

This activity will be followed up in the science activities of the Winter and Spring themes.

1. *Measure heights*: Find a permanent, erect object such as a fence post or street sign. Measure its height. Do not use children's heights; they tend to grow and throw off subsequent measurements.

2. *Measure time*: Determine the exact "midday" by finding the times of sunrise and sunset, calculating the number of hours of daylight, and dividing in half.

FOR EXAMPLE: If the sun rises at 7:15 and sets at 6:45, that's 11 hours and 30 minutes of daylight. Half that amount is 5 hours and 45 minutes. 7:15 plus 5:45 equals 13:00 or 1:00 p.m. (Older children can do this calculation themselves.)

3. *Measure lengths*: At exact midday, measure the length of the shadow cast by the object. Do not use a simple clock time (such as noon on September 21, December 21 and March 21) because daylight savings will cause gross inaccuracies.

Math/Science

4. Save the measurements you take because you will need them in Winter. Younger children may stop here while older children continue with the geometry.

5. Calculate the amount of daylight for the first day of autumn at exact midday.

6. *Measure angles*: Older children may plot the angle of the sun by using graph paper to draw a scale model. The object forms one side of the angle, the shadow forms the base, and an imaginary line from the top of the object to the tip of the shadow forms the hypotenuse. Compare these angles for autumn, winter, and spring.

7. *Calculate ratios*: Find the ratio of object height to shadow length. FOR EXAMPLE: If the stop sign is 240 cm high and the shadow is 80 cm long, the "object to shadow ratio" is 240:80 or 3:1.

What Are My Stats?

NAME _____

I have a problem. Coach says I'm supposed to figure out my career stats, but I'm really awful at Math. Can you help me?

TD = Touchdowns

PA = Pass Attempts

PC = Pass Completions

YEAR	TD	PA	PC	%
Year 1	27	254	127	50%
Year 2	29	294	160	_____
Year 3	41	368	184	_____
Year 4	Didn't play	0	0	_____
Year 5	19	196	78	_____
Year 6	26	287	185	_____
Year 7	26	365	224	_____
Year 8	32	464	365	_____
Total	_____	_____	_____	_____
Average	_____	_____	_____	_____

1. Find the percent of pass completions each year by dividing the number of completed passes by the number of pass attempts. (127 divided by 254 is 50%). Use a calculator.

2. Find the averages by adding the columns and dividing by **7** (the number of years he played).

Autumn

Sunrise and Sunset

NAME _____

Date	High	Low	Sunrise	Sunset
Sept 23	68	45	7:01 A.M.	7:11 P.M.
Sept 30	65	42	7:09 A.M.	6:56 P.M.
Oct 7	63	40	7:07 A.M.	6:12 P.M.
Oct 14	61	39	7:27 A.M.	6:30 P.M.
Oct 21	58	36	7:33 A.M.	6:22 P.M.
Oct 28	51	31	7:46 A.M.	6:07 P.M.
Nov 4	48	29	7:55 A.M.	5:58 P.M.
Nov 11	44	27	8:02 A.M.	5:41 P.M.
Nov 18	39	21	8:14 A.M.	5:42 P.M.
Nov 25	35	18	8:23 A.M.	5:37 P.M.

1. Make a graph to show how the Highs and Lows change during Autumn.

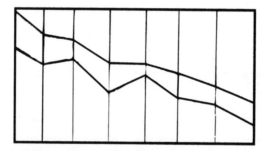

2. Make a graph to show how the length of daylight shrinks during autumn.

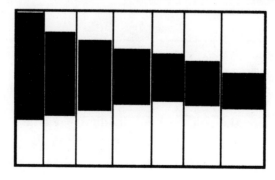

© 1995 by The Center for Applied Research in Education

NAME _____

November Elections

Directions:

Elections are always held in November. This year Betty Cheets and Seymour Cash ran for Congress. The results are just coming in. Who is ahead? Who do you think will win?

Town	For CASH	For CHEETS	Winner
Boilington	Not in	Not in	
Cannon Falls	1,444	2,569	Cheets
Monkey Mills	3,396	1,996	
Big Toe Flats	Not in	Not in	
Drizzly Creek	661	883	
Sour Lake	40	99	
Foggy Ridge	2,749	2,491	
Frost Meadow	2,111	1,959	
Little Spain	Not in	Not in	
Banana Splits	2,659	2,777	
TOTALS	_____	_____	

Who do think will win? _____

Why do you think so? _____

_____

_____

All Hallow's Evening
(a teacher-led activity)

Purpose:
The customs of Halloween come from a variety of different traditions and most had very serious meanings. Here are explanations of the customs.

The Black Cat
The Celts of ancient Ireland celebrated a festival on the last day of October called Samhain. This festival was a way of saying goodbye to summer. They believed that on this night the souls of the year's dead returned to Earth for a final foray in the form of animals.

Trick-or-Treat
The Celts also had a custom of wearing masks and begging for food door to door. People gave food to appease the god Muck Olla. This god would be angered and visit ill fortune on the family that refused to give food to the visitors.

Jack-of-the-Lantern (Jack-o'-Lantern)
An old Irish tale tells of a mean and mischievous man named Jack who was pursued by the Devil. The Devil wanted Jack's soul. Jack tricked him into climbing a tree, and then trapped him there by painting a cross on the tree. The Devil moaned and promised not to take Jack's soul if he would let him down. Jack did, and feeling certain he was forever free of the devil, went back to his old mean and rotten ways. When Jack died he was not welcomed into Heaven because he had lived a wicked life, so he went to the Devil. The Devil reminded Jack of his promise not to take his soul, and chased him away by chucking a burning coal at him. Jack kept the coal to use as a light, but put it in a hollow turnip to keep from burning his hands. Now he wanders the Earth with his turnip lantern looking for a place to rest. OOOOOOOooooooooOOOOoo!!!

Bats

Dracula was a count in old Hungary. He really was a mean fellow, but he didn't drink blood and couldn't turn into a bat. In fact, that's an insult to bats. Most bats eat fruits and bugs (lots of bugs, so be thankful). There are vampire bats, though, and it's true that they prefer to play at night. But they usually bite animals and drink only about an ounce of blood. No one ever turns into a bat, but you can get rabies from them.

Apple Bobbing

The Celts thought of the apple as a magical fruit and since it is usually harvested in fall, it has become a part of Halloween. The Celtic game of apple bobbing was different though. They tied an apple to a string suspended from the ceiling. Participants tried to "snap up" the apple without using their hands. Whoever got hold of the apple with his or her mouth won it. Try this game in your classroom.

A Multicultural Harvest Festival
(a teacher-led activity)

Purpose:

Many cultures have festivals to give thanks for the harvest. Good harvests were especially important in the early days when people needed to store huge amounts of food for winter. The more bountiful the harvest, the more comfortable the coming winter would be.

Have a multicultural harvest festival! After explaining each ancient and traditional festival, permit children to share a small piece of that tradition.

The Harvest Meal

1. Talk about our Thanksgiving traditions. This is the harvest festival of the United States and Canada. Like most traditional harvest festivals, we sample all the delicious things the Good Earth has yielded. Nearly every harvest festival has this same tradition. So don't feel guilty. Humans have been overindulging at harvest time for centuries!

2. Explain the Chinese Festival of the Eighth Moon. The eighth moon, occurring sometime in late August or early September, was the "harvest moon." The full moon provided the extra light needed for the long hours of work to harvest the crops. One tradition during this festival is the eating of round rice cakes (shaped like the full moon). These were typically made from the rice harvested that year, but you can get an ample supply at the grocery store.

3. The Ancient Greeks had a festival to honor the goddess Demeter who was patroness of the harvest. This celebration lasted a little over a week (imagine eating Thanksgiving Dinner almost constantly for eight or nine days!). Among the other traditions was a ceremonial eating of fruit and nuts and the drinking of rich, red grape wine. Make GORP (Good Old Raisins and Peanuts: 1 part raisins to 1 part peanuts. Mix well.). Put spoonfuls in muffin cups, and set them beside the rice cakes. Purple grape juice will round out the meal.

4. In many North and South American cultures, wheat and corn were the essential crops. It has been customary in many American cultures to adorn the home with so-called "Indian Corn" (the corn with colorful yellow, white, and brown kernels). This is dried and hung on doorposts in the autumn to welcome the corn spirit. Decorate the room with "Indian Corn." Leave the husks on them though. Add corn flakes to your harvest festival. Try finding blue corn flakes or blue cornmeal in health food shops or the organic food section of your grocery store.

5. In Europe the last sheaf of wheat harvested was kept in a special place, where the people believed the spirit of the wheat lived. Sometimes it was dried in the barn and burned in spring in hope of a good growing season. You'll want to add wheat to the meal. Puffed wheat (the kind without the "golden" sugar-laden glaze) makes a nice addition. This was a traditional food in ancient Europe and the recipe was actually given to them by Roman soldiers.

The Last of the Patuxet

A Play
by Karl A. Matz

Characters:

Squanto, the last of the Patuxet
Wampanoag Friend
2 Patuxet elders
Sir Fernando
English Teacher
Captain John Smith
The Spanish Sailor
Slave buyer
Massasoit, the Wampanoag Elder

Narrator:	It is dawn in the forest. Fourteen-year-old Squanto is hunting for deer with a spear. (*Squanto is hiding behind a tree. Suddenly a Friend from the Wampanoag people comes running up.*)
Wampanoag Friend:	Squanto! You must go quickly! Strange men have come to your village.
Squanto:	(*He's frustrated with her.*) Look what you've done! You've scared away the deer I was stalking.
Wampanoag Friend:	Never mind that. You must go. These men have skin like snow and hair on their faces!
Squanto:	Hair on their faces? Don't be silly. People don't grow hair on their faces!

Wampanoag Friend:	These men do and they carry sticks that make thunder and lightning. You must go now.
Squanto:	I will go, but only to show you what a fool you are.
Narrator:	But when Squanto returned to his village he saw the men his friend had described. They were strange looking and spoke a funny language that sounded to Squanto like the grunts of hungry pigs. The leader of the whites was talking to the elders of the village. He was acting out his strange words, trying to make the Patuxet people understand.
Sir Fernando:	*(speaking slowly and acting out his words with big actions)* We will give you many beads and buttons. You will give us furs.
Patuxet Elder I:	*(to Elder II)* I think he wants to give us those toys for our furs. He must be crazy. *(to Sir Fernando also acting out)* We will give you furs, but you give us tools and knives.
Sir Fernando:	*(speaking slow and acting out)* You want tools? You must give more in trade. *(He grabs Squanto.)* I will take him.
Patuxet Elder II:	You will go with this crazy person to his land. When you come back you can tell us where he comes from and what his land is like.
Squanto:	I will.
Narrator:	So Squanto went to England with Sir Fernando.
Sir Fernando:	*(to English Teacher)* This is Squanto. Teach him English so I can find out where the best trapping and hunting lands are. He will be my ticket to RICHES!
English Teacher:	Squanto. This is hand. Hand.
Squanto:	Haaaaaaannnnnnnndddd.
English Teacher:	GOOD! Hand. This is arm.
Squanto:	Arm. *(Squanto sits facing the English teacher in a silent pantomime of the English lesson as the Narrator speaks.)*
Narrator:	Squanto learned to speak English and lived in England for nine years. His life was good in England

but he was lonesome and wanted to go home. He heard that Captain John Smith was planning a trip soon.

Captain Smith: Yes, Squanto, I am planning a trip to the New World. Why?

Squanto: I would like to come with you. I think it is time to return to my people.

Captain Smith: Well, I am actually landing north of your village. It would take several days to walk to your village from there.

Squanto (*very happy*): That's all right. I don't mind walking. When do you leave?

Captain Smith: First thing tomorrow morning.

Squanto: I will be ready. Thank you. (*Squanto and Captain Smith hunt in the background as Narrator speaks.*)

Narrator: Captain Smith hoped to find gold, but there was none. Squanto suggested that they hunt and trap furs to take back to England so the trip wouldn't be a complete waste.

Captain Smith: Squanto, you've really saved the day. I now have more than enough furs to pay for the trip. I guess you will want to get home now.

Squanto: Yes, I had better go. Winter is coming and I will need time to prepare. (*As the narrator speaks, the actions he or she describes are acted out by the actors.*)

Narrator: The two men parted ways and Squanto headed for home. But before he could get back, he was captured by Spanish sailors who tied him up and took him to Spain.

Spanish Sailor: Who wants to buy this strong young Indian? He can do hard work and will give you many strong children to use as slaves.

Slave Buyer: I will buy him. I have many big rocks to move and I need a strong slave for that. (*gives the sailor money and hauls Squanto away on a leash*)

Narrator: Poor Squanto! For many long years he worked as a slave in Spain. Life was very hard and Squanto decided at last that he must escape or he would never see his people and his land again. He escaped one night and found a job on a ship headed for England. He met an English Captain and got a job on his ship to the New World. The ship landed in Newfoundland, a large island in Canada. He had to walk back home. He had lived through many years in England and Spain. Many years of loneliness and hard work, but now Squanto came to the same forest in which he had once hunted deer. He was home.

Squanto: *(happily)* There through the trees, I can see the village. The people will be so glad to see me! *(Squanto steps closer. His happiness changes to sadness.)* No one is here. Where has everyone gone?

Wampanoag Friend: *(older now also)* Squanto? Is that you?

Squanto: Yes! It's me. Tell me. Where have all my people gone?

Wampanoag Friend: Dead. There was a horrible sickness brought by the whites. The old people and small children went first, but one by one the people all died like grasses falling in the wind.

Squanto: Where will I go now? What will I do? I am the last of the Patuxet people.

Wampanoag Friend: Come to my village with me. We will talk to Massasoit the chief. Maybe he will invite you to live with us.

Narrator: So Squanto went to live among the Wampanoag people. Life was good, but Squanto was lonely. He kept to himself, until one day when Massasoit sent for him.

Massasoit: Squanto. I want to speak with you.

Squanto: *(he sounds sad)* Yes. What do you want?

Massasoit: There is a ship off the coast. It carries white people. My hunters saw them yesterday. They have come ashore and are building a village.

Squanto: I do not know anything about that.

Massasoit: No, how could you? You lay in your house all day and speak to no one.

Squanto: That is my business.

Massasoit: Yes, you're right. That is your business. Your friend, the one who brought you here, told me that you know how to make the grunting talk of the white people.

Squanto: The whites have many languages. I know English and Spanish.

Massasoit: You will go to these people. Find out what they want. Find out if they have guns and if they are many in number. I want to know if we have new neighbors or new enemies.

Squanto: Very well. I will do that. Where are they building their village?

Massasoit: They are camping right on the very spot where your village used to be!

Narrator: So Squanto walked into the forest to meet the Pilgrims. You know the rest of the story.

The End

Autumn

Apple People

Materials:

One big apple (green or red) for each child
Knives (butter knives are safe and work just fine)
Apple corer
Salt water
Yarn and other accessories

Procedure:

1. Look carefully at the apple. Decide where to put the nose.
2. CAREFULLY cut away the eyes and the space under the nose.
3. Cut a long deep mouth.
4. Carefully add features such as wrinkles, smile lines, and eyebrows.
5. Core the apple and let stand until it begins to wrinkle.
6. When it is brown and wrinkled just the way you like it, soak the apple in salt water for 30-40 minutes. Put it someplace safe and warm to dry overnight.
7. Add yarn hair, fabric hats and other accessories to give your wrinkled apple person some character.

Br-r-r-r!

Start off by reading to the class *Frederick* by Leo Leonni. Frederick saved the joys and feelings of summer to share with his friends during the cold gray months of winter. A celebration of summer in the depths of winter always helps to lighten the long doldrums between winter break and spring break. Invite the children to brainstorm by asking, "What are some things we could do to remember summer?" Here are some activities and ideas, inspired by Frederick's genius!

1. Eat popsicles, fruit cocktail, ice cream, snow cones, drink lemonade.

2. Listen to music by the Beach Boys.

3. Read summer books. (You'll find a bibliography in the Summer theme section.)

4. Write about "What I did on my summer vacation."

5. Have a beach party, complete with beach towels, sunglasses, and tongs.

6. Make flowers for an art project, or better still . . . Plant real flowers, if you have access to a sunny window.

7. Here's a recipe for a fun summer shake that you can make in the dead of winter. You need one 16-oz. can of peaches (with juice), a pint of vanilla yogurt, and some ice. Put all ingredients in a blender and mix to a froth. Makes eight 4-oz. servings (just a taste!).

Bulletin Board Idea

# Bibliography

Ahlberg, A. *The Black Cat.* **New York: Greenwillow Books, 1990. (unpaged).** A Halloween kind of winter book! A black cat watches the foolish behavior of three skeletons who are out sledding in the snow.

Bauer, C. *Midnight Snowman.* **New York: Athenum, 1987. (32 pages).** Especially for those who live in places where snow rarely falls. In a somewhat more southerly community, a neighborhood bands together to build a snowman before an unusual snowfall turns to rain.

Briggs, R. *The Snowman.* **New York: Random House, 1978. (32 pages).** When his snowman comes to life, a little boy invites him home. In return, the snowman takes the boy on a fantastic flight high above the countryside.

Butterworth, N. *One Snowy Night.* **Boston: Little, Brown & Co., 1990. (25 pages).** One snowy night a park employee brings all the park animals into his hut to keep warm. The hut is too tiny and that's how the trouble begins.

Carlson, N. L. *Take Time to Relax.* **New York: Viking, 1991. (32 pages).** A story of a busy family of beavers who must take time to relax when a storm leaves them snowbound.

Carlstrom, N. *The Snow Speaks.* **Boston: Little, Brown & Co., 1992. (unpaged.)** A book of sights and sounds of the season's first snowfall.

Carlstrom, N. *Goodbye, Geese.* **New York: Philomel, 1992.** A father and his little girl look skyward and search for signs of the coming winter.

Chorao, K. *Kate's Snowman.* **New York: EP Dutton, 1982. (22 pages).** Kate makes a snowman that has the characteristics of members of her family.

Frost, R. *Stopping by the Woods on a Snowy Evening.* **New York: EP Dutton, 1978\. (26 pages).** A beautiful picture book version of Frost's immortal poem. Don't pass this one up!

George, W. *Winter at Long Pond.* **New York: Trumpet, 1992. (28 pages).** A boy and his father look at all the wonders of winter while on a trip to chop down a spruce tree. The artwork depicting wildlife in winter is absolutely breathtaking!

Goffstein, M. *Our Snowman.* **New York: Harper & Row, 1986. (25 pages).** Two children build a snowman, but he looks so lonely at night that the little girl and her father decide to build him a wife.

Greene, C. *Ice is . . . Whee!* **Chicago: Children's Press, A Rookie Reader, 1983. (31 pages).** Two boys enjoy an icy morning. They explore ice through sight, touch, and kinesthetic experiences.

Hader, B., and Hader, E. *The Big Snow.* **New York: Collier Books, 1948. (43 pages).** The Caldecott-winning story of animals in a forest preparing for the coming of winter.

Harshman, M. *The Snow Company.* **New York: Cobblehill Books, 1991. (28 pages).** The unexpected excitement of a houseful of people who become stranded together during a blizzard.

Hidaka, M. *Girl from the Snow Country.* **New York: Kane/Miller, 1986. (31 pages).** A Japanese girl plays in the falling snow as she and her mother walk across a wide field to the market.

Keats, E. J. *The Snowy Day.* **New York: Viking, 1962. (28 pages).** A little boy wanders outside after a major snowfall and plays alone while the bigger kids have a snowball fight. A classic!

Keller, H. *Geraldine's Big Snow.* **New York: Greenwillow Books, 1988. (26 pages).** Geraldine is anxious for the first snowfall so she can go sledding.

Kessler, E. *The Day Daddy Stayed Home.* **Middletown, CT: Weekly Reader Books, 1959. (unpaged).** A horrible blizzard closes all the schools and businesses so Daddy stays home and plays in the snow with the children. Reflects the family and homelife of the late 1950's.

London, J. *Froggy Gets Dressed.* **New York: Viking, 1992. (unpaged).** Froggy wants to play outside in the snow but gets called back by his mother for some necessary articles of clothing.

Loretan, S. *Bob the Snowman.* **New York: Penguin, 1988. (25 pages).** One snowy day some neighborhood children made a snowman they named Bob. Bob was happy, but then came the day he had to move south for the winter.

Madokor, H. *Buster's First Snow.* **New York: Garth Stevens, 1991. (24 pages).** Buster and Snapper are puppies who find a lost mitten in the snow and track down its owner.

Neitzel, S. *The Jacket That I Wear in the Snow.* **New York: Greenwillow, 1989. (32 pages).** A rhyming book in which a little girl names all the things she must wear to play in the snow.

Van Allsburg, C. *The Polar Express.* **New York: Houghton-Mifflin, 1985. (30 pages).** If any children's book of the 1980's becomes a classic, this one will. A story of a magical train that runs from "here" to the North Pole.

Vigna, J. *Boot Weather.* **New York: A. Whitman, 1989. (32 pages).** A very imaginative little girl playing in the snow creates all kinds of wonderful adventures.

Ward, A. *Baby Bear and the Big Sleep.* **Boston: Little, Brown & Co., 1980. (32 pages).** A knee slapper about how the youngest member of a family of bears puts off going to sleep for the winter. A must for read-aloud.

Watson, W. *Has Winter Come?* **New York: William Collins, 1978. (unpaged).** The story of a woodchuck family's preparations for the long winter ahead.

Watanabe, S. *Ice Cream Is Falling!* **New York: Philomel, 1989. (34 pages.)** Bear and his friends have fun playing in the falling snow.

Ziefert, H. *Snow Magic.* **New York: Viking Kestrel, 1988. (36 pages).** The snow people have a party when the first snowfall comes on the first day of winter.

Zolotow, C. *Something Is Going to Happen.* **New York: Harper & Row, 1988. (unpaged).** While her family sleeps, a little girl is overcome with a feeling that something special is going to happen. And it does. As the family wakes they are greeted to the beautiful sight of gently falling snow.

WINTER BOOKS I'VE READ

1. _____ Title _____
   _____ Author _____
2. _____ Title _____
   _____ Author _____
3. _____ Title _____
   _____ Author _____
4. _____ Title _____
   _____ Author _____
5. _____ Title _____
   _____ Author _____

NAME_____

Has Winter Come?
by
Wendy Watson

NAME _____

1. What are three things the family in this story did to get ready for winter?

   _____

   _____

   _____

2. Name three things YOU must do to get ready for winter.

   _____

   _____

   _____

3. The children in the story could not tell that winter was coming. What are some ways YOU can tell that winter is on the way?

   _____

   _____

   _____

4. The children in the story drank hot cider and ate popcorn. What do YOU like to eat and drink when it's cold outside?

   _____

   _____

   _____

Reading

Kate's Snowman
by
Kay Chorao

NAME _____

Directions:

Make this Snow Person look like someone in your family. On the back of the page, tell who it is and why you drew it the way you did.

Reading/Arts and Crafts

The Big Snow
by
Berta and Elmer Hader

NAME _____

Directions:

Fill out the STORY MAP below as the story is read aloud to you.

Where did it happen?	To whom did it happen?
When did it happen?	
What happened?	**How did it end?**
Did you like it?	**Why?**

NAME _____

Winter Words

Directions:
Try to think of one winter word for each letter of the alphabet. How many can you do?

A _____   N _____

B _____   O _____

C _____   P _____

D _____   Q _____

E _____   R _____

F _____   S _____

G _____   T _____

H _____   U _____

I _____   V _____

J _____   W _____

K _____   X _____

L _____   Y _____

M _____   Z _____

Language Arts

NAME _____

Winter Writing Warmup

5 THINGS I LIKE ABOUT WINTER
(Use complete sentences.)

1._____

2._____

3._____

4._____

5._____

5 THINGS I DON'T LIKE ABOUT WINTER
(Use complete sentences.)

1._____

2._____

3._____

4._____

5._____

Language Arts

White Is Winter

by Karl A. Matz

White is Winter
Ice and Snow.
Red are my cheeks when the cold winds blow.
Blue is my window
With its frosty light.
Black is a blizzard on a stormy night.
Brown are the little birds
pecking for seeds.
Grey are the icicles jingling from the weeds.
Oh, where did the colors of summertime go?
They are hiding very quietly
Underneath the snow.

Winter Is a Waiting Time

by Karl A. Matz

Winter is a waiting time,
A time for wishes and dreams
of Summer's blue and Autumn's gold
and Spring's exploding greens.
The joy of winter is waiting
For the times we love the best,
For dreaming of swimming and baseball games
While we give our bones a rest.
Oh, but the pond is smooth with ice
and the hills are white with snow.
Winter is a playing time,
Don't sit there! Get up! Let's go!

What Will the Birdies Do Then, the Poor Things?

Anonymous

The North Wind Doth Blow
And we shall have snow
And what will the birdies do then, the poor things?
Oh, what will the birdies do then, the poor things?
They'll sit in the barn
to keep themselves warm
And tuck their heads under their wings, the poor things
And tuck their heads under their wings, the poor things.
The North Wind Doth Blow
And we shall have snow
And what will the birdies do then, the poor things?
Oh, what will the birdies do then, the poor things?
Roll up in a ball
in their nests snug and small
And tuck their heads under their wings, the poor things
And tuck their heads under their wings, the poor things.
The North Wind Doth Blow
And we shall have snow
And what will the birdies do then, the poor things?
Oh, what will the birdies do then, the poor things?
They'll fly to the south
With a worm in their mouths
And tuck their heads under their wings, the poor things
And tuck their heads under their wings, the poor things.

Other Poetry Resources

From Shel Silverstein:

A Light in the Attic
Here Comes (page 32)
Come Skating (page 71)

Where the Sidewalk Ends
Snowman (page 65)
Santa and the Reindeer (page 90)
Merry . . . (page 164)

From *Sing a Song of Popcorn: Every Child's Book of Poems*

I Heard a Bird Sing by Oliver Herford (page 20)
The More It Snows and Furry Bear by A. A. Milne (page 22)
Sing a Song of Popcorn by Nancy Byrd Turner (page 23)
Snowflakes by David Cord (page 24)
First Snow by Marie Allen (page 25)
Winter Moon by Langston Hughes (page 124)
Snow Melting by Ruth Krauss (page 132)
Snow by Issa (page 133)

Language Arts

Puppet Show
(a teacher-led activity)

Puppet shows have the advantage of integrating art with reading and oral language.

Materials:

A ruler or long stick

White construction paper

White cardstock (optional)

Colored construction paper scraps

Fabric pieces, ric-rac and ribbon (optional)

Glue

Crayons

Scissors

Procedure:

1. Make copies of the snowperson pattern on the following page. Copy onto white cardstock, if possible.
2. Invite children to color and decorate their snowkids to give them character and personality. This must be done before the snowpersons are assembled.
3. Glue the body onto the front of the stick. Glue the arms on the side.
4. Add accessories such as hats, hair, shirts, scarves, etc. Wait until the glue is dry before adding anything to the puppet.
5. Have the class pick two boy puppets and two girl puppets. These four, however you choose them, will be the cast for the following puppet show, *The Snow Kids*.

Language Arts

Snowperson Pattern

The Snow Kids

A Puppet Play
by Karl A. Matz

Characters:

Connie

Gina

Bobby

Sanford

(The four puppets are standing still and quiet as snow people do. Gradually we hear a muffled whisper.)

Bobby: Hey! Hey! Can you guys hear me?

Connie: I hear you. Be quiet. You're a snowkid. You're not supposed to talk!

Bobby: Well, neither are you!

Sanford: You two quit arguing. Someone might hear!

Bobby: I don't care who hears. I'm sick and tired of standing around all day like . . . like . . .

Gina: Like a snowkid?

Bobby: Yeah! I want to be FREE! I want adventure.

Gina: Adventure? Like what? You're made of snowballs!

Bobby: Well—Don't you ever wonder what's over there?

Sanford: You mean over that hill by that green house?

Bobby: Yeah! I've been standing here for days, freezing my carrot nose off, and just staring at that hill. I'm sick of it. I want to see what's on the other side.

Sanford: But what if it's something dangerous?

Connie: Yeah! There could be something hot that would melt you.

Sanford: Or maybe some water! If you fell in, you'd be slush!

Gina: Do you think you could do it, Bobby?

Bobby: If I could, would you come, too?

Gina: You bet! I'm sick of just standing here, too.

Connie: GINA! What are you saying?

Gina: Come on, Connie. Aren't you just a little curious?

Bobby: Well, if you want to go, then let's get started!

Gina: How can we?

Sanford and Connie: You can't!

Bobby: *(groaning as if trying to lift something heavy)* UUUHHH-HGGGG!

Gina: What are you doing?

Sanford: Stop it, man!

Connie: You're scaring me.

Bobby: UUUUUNNNNNGGGGG!

Gina: You moved, Bobby. I saw it!

Bobby: *(working hard)* You've got to get yourself rolling a little.

Connie: How do you know this?

Bobby: I've done it before!

Connie: *(angry)* When?

Gina: *(thrilled)* Yeah! When?

Sanford: I know. It was last night. I saw you. You went out to the street and back.

Bobby: You could have told on me and you didn't! What a pal!

Sanford: Who would I tell? I'm a snowkid.

Bobby: You've got a point. Well, just a little more. *(breaks free)* THERE! Here I go! Who's coming?

Gina: ME! UUUUUNNNNNGGGG! OOOWWWW! UMPH! I'm free! Bye, Connie! Bye, Sanford! *(Bobby disappears)* Wait, Bobby! Wait for me!

Connie: GINA Q. SNOWKID, YOU GET BACK HERE THIS INSTANT!

(Gina disappears following right behind Bobby.)

Sanford: Come on, Connie. Let's go with them.

Connie: But you never know what could happen over there!

Sanford: I know what's going to happen here. We'll stand here until March and turn into a pile of slush, then we'll be gone. That's if some kid doesn't kick us over first. No thanks! I'm leaving.

Connie: Sanford, NO!

Sanford: UUUUMMMMPH! OOOFFF! Just——got——to——get—— rolling! UMPH! THERE!

Connie: Sanford, STOP!

Sanford: Bye, Connie! I'm off to see what's on the other side of the hill.

Connie: But what if someone sees you? *(Sanford is gone.)* Sanford? *(long silence).* Sanford? Bobby? GINNNNNAAAAAA! Heey, you guys! Wait for me! UUUUUGGGHHHHHHH! How'd they do that? HEY? OOOOOFFFFFF! HERE I COME! *(she disappears)*

THE END

An "Icy" Experiment
(a teacher-led activity)

One of the hardest weather concepts to teach young children is the way in which the uneven heating and cooling of the Earth causes winds. A simple science demonstration can do the trick.

Materials:
Each group will need a pint jar or large glass of warm water, an ice cube made from colored water, and a copy of the worksheet for this activity.

Procedure:

1. Divide the class into groups of four. One child will be the scribe.

2. Tell the students that they will soon place the colored ice cube into the glass of warm water. Ask them to discuss among themselves what will happen as the ice cube melts. The scribe records their predictions on part 1 of the worksheet.

3. The ice cube is placed in the glass. Children will observe as the ice cube melts, that the cooler water sinks to the bottom of the glass and spreads outward along the bottom. These observations are discussed and then recorded in part 2.

4. Give children the following premise: "Suppose it is a warm day in fall, and a bubble of cold air is high above our town." In groups the class predicts then records their predictions in part 3. Guide them to the understanding that the cooler air will sink and spread out across the land as a cold wind, while the warmer air rises to make room. That day will become cold and windy.

An "Icy" Experiment

Worksheet

Group Members: _____

1. **PREDICT.** In a moment you will place a colored ice cube in a glass of warm water. In your group, discuss what will happen as the ice cube melts. Record your predictions below.

   _____
   _____
   _____
   _____

2. **OBSERVE.** Place the ice cube into the warm water and watch as the ice cube begins to melt. As a group, discuss what is happening and record your observations below.

   _____
   _____
   _____
   _____

3. **EXTEND.** Listen to your teacher's directions. As a group, discuss what happens when cold air is high in the sky on a warm autumn day. How does the ice cube experiment help to explain this?

   _____
   _____
   _____
   _____

NAME _____

A Cool Science Problem

Group Members:

_____

_____

What Do You Think:

1. In what kind of water will an ice cube melt faster—saltwater or fresh water?

   Our group believes that:

   ❏ the ice cube will melt faster in the fresh water.

   ❏ the ice cube will melt faster in the salt water.

   ❏ the ice cubes will melt the same in both kinds of water.

   ❏ the ice cubes will not melt.

2. We believe this because _____
   _____
   _____

3. Here's how we tested our idea: _____
   _____
   _____

4. Here's what happened: _____
   _____
   _____

The Winter Solstice
(a teacher-led activity)

Concept:

Observe the astronomical changes of winter.

You need:

Metersticks
A sunny day
The weather report from today's paper

Procedure:

This activity is a follow-up of a science activity in the Autumn theme and will be followed up again in the Spring theme.

1. **Measure heights:** Find the permanent, erect object that you used in Autumn. Measure or recall its height. Do not use children's heights; they tend to grow and throw off subsequent measurements.

2. **Measure time:** Determine the exact "midday" by finding the times of sunrise and sunset, calculating the number of hours of daylight and dividing in half.

FOR EXAMPLE: If the sun rises at 7:15 and sets at 6:45, that's 11 hours and 30 minutes of daylight. Half that amount is 5 hours and 45 minutes. 7:15 plus 5:45 equals 13:00 or 1:00 P.M. (Older children can do this calculation themselves.)

3. **Measure lengths:** At exact midday, measure the length of the shadow cast by the object. Do not use a simple clock time (such as noon on September 21, December 21, and March 21) because daylight savings will cause gross inaccuracies.

4. Save the measurements you take because you will need them in Spring. Compare the length of the shadows measured in Autumn and Winter. How much different are they? Why are they different? Younger children may stop here while older children continue with the geometry.

5. Calculate the amount of daylight for the first day of winter at exact mid day. Compare the amount of daylight and the time of midday with those figures calculated in Autumn.

6. **Measure angles:** Older children may plot the angle of the declination of the Sun by using graph paper to draw a scale model. The object will form one side of the angle, the shadow forms the base, and an imaginary line from the top of the object to the tip of the shadow forms the hypotenuse. Compare this angle for autumn and winter.

7. **Calculate ratios:** Find the ratio of object height to shadow length. FOR EXAMPLE: If the stop sign is 240 cm high and the shadow is 80 cm long the "object to shadow ratio" is 240:80 or 3:1.

Snowpeople Arithmetic

Directions:
Complete each problem by putting a plus, minus or multiplication sign in the square. Be careful—don't slip!

NAME _____

Story Problems

Directions:

Finish the table below and answer the questions that follow.

Snowfall in Denver, CO, This Winter

November	3 inches
December	6 inches
January	11 inches
February	14 inches
March	7 inches
April	1 inch

1. During which month was the snowfall the heaviest?

    _____

2. During which month was the snowfall the lightest?

    _____

3. How much more snow fell during the heaviest month compared to the the lightest month?

    _____

4. What was the total accumulation of snow during this winter?

    _____

5. What was the total amount of snow that fell by December 31?

    _____

BONUS:

What was the AVERAGE monthly snowfall during this winter? Which month's snowfall came closest to the average?

    _____

Using Winter Count
(a teacher-led activity)

Materials:

Transparency or enlarged version of the completed "Winter Count"
Sufficient copies of the blank "Winter Count" sheet for each student
Markers or crayons

Procedure:

1. Show the model of Winter Count to the class and explain that the winter count was a traditional way in which the Native American people of the Plains recorded the important events in the life of the community. A symbol was chosen to represent the single most important event of the year, which they measured from winter to winter. This symbol was painted on a specially prepared skin. The earliest symbols were in the middle; each year, the symbols spiraled outward in a circular, clockwise direction. The circle was sacred because it represented life to the Plains people: eternal and without end.

2. Invite the class to offer their suggestions concerning the meaning of the symbols on the enlarged Winter Count.

   (1) an especially plentiful buffalo hunt
   (2) death of an important leader
   (3) a year of drought
   (4) a war with a neighboring group
   (5) moving the village to a new place
   (6) a wet and rainy year
   (7) a plentiful hunt
   (8) an important visitor who came by canoe
   (9) a white trader visits
   (10) a year when many horses were obtained

   Point out that the Winter Count contains both happy events and sad events.

3. Inform the students that they will be creating winter counts of their own lives. Explain that it takes careful planning to choose the most important event from a year and to select just the right symbol. To the Plains peoples, this was especially important because the Winter Count was displayed in a prominent place for all to see. Explain to the class that their

winter counts will be displayed also, and that class members will be asked to try to read them when they are done.

4. Brainstorm and list the seminal events in the children's lives. As children begin to suggest important events ("I broke my arm when I was three," "We moved to a new town," "I got my dog"), other children's memories will be nudged and they will think of similar events. Write these on the chalkboard or the overhead projector as they are offered and make them accessible while the children are working.

5. Pass out the blank Winter Count page and explain to the children that they will start in the middle with a big event from their first year and spiral outward and clockwise. Remind the children to make the symbols colorful. You may wish to give children a day to consult with parents or send the sheet home and ask parents to help the children remember and select those important events.

6. When the Winter Count is completed, you may wish to pair children and have them try to read one another's lives. Then mount the Winter Counts on brown paper (to represent the wooden frames the Plains people used) and display them in a prominent place in the room or hallway.

A Completed Winter Count

NAME _____

My Winter Count

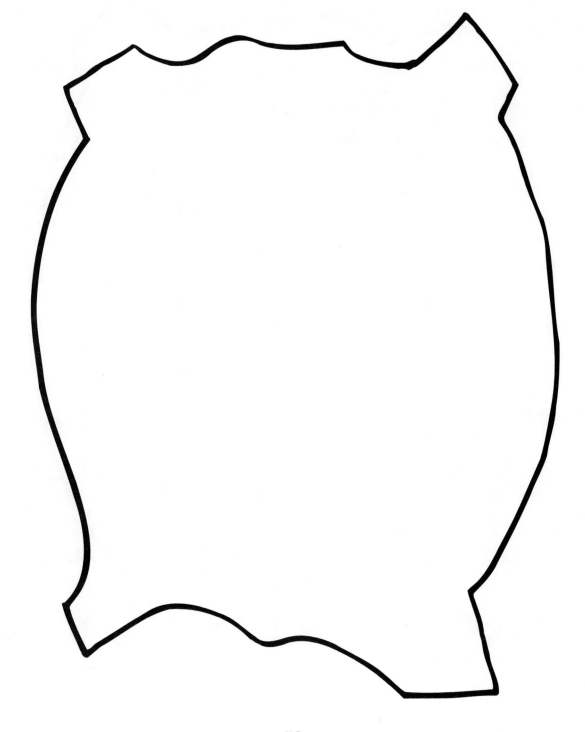

NAME _____

The Truth About Eskimos

Directions:
The statements below are some things that people think about Eskimos. Read about Eskimos and find out which of the statements are true and which are myths.

1. Eskimos live in igloos made from blocks of ice.   TRUE   MYTH

2. Eskimos used to hunt and eat seals.   TRUE   MYTH

3. Today many Eskimos go hunting on snowmobiles.   TRUE   MYTH

4. Eskimos live only in Alaska.   TRUE   MYTH

5. "Inuit" is the official name of the Eskimo people.   TRUE   MYTH

6. The people of the Aleutian Islands in Southern Alaska are related to the Eskimo people.   TRUE   MYTH

7. "Eskimo" means "People who eat raw meat." That's because Eskimos eat raw polar bear meat.   TRUE   MYTH

8. The Eskimos probably came to North America from Russia by traveling across the Bering Strait.   TRUE   MYTH

9. Eskimos have strong family relationships.   TRUE   MYTH

10. Eskimo boats are called "kayaks."   TRUE   MYTH

NAME _____

Is Your State Blue or Green?

Directions:
Some states have cold and snowy winters, and others do not. Find the average temperature for January for your state and nine others. Write them on the states below. If that is a winter state, color it blue. If it is not, color it green.

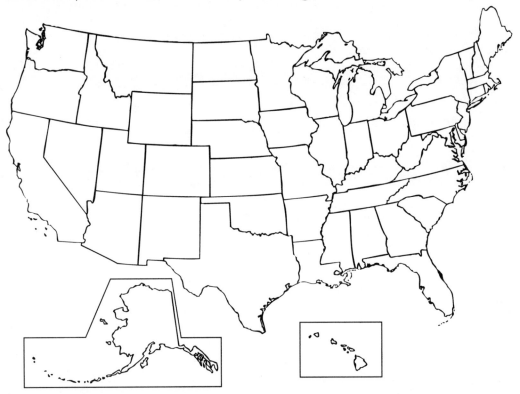

1. Name the coldest state of the ten you chose. _____

2. Why do you think this state is so cold? _____

3. Name the warmest state of the ten you chose. _____

4. Why do you think this state is so warm? _____

_____

Snowglobes
(a teacher-led activity)

Those little glass balls with the snowstorms inside have always been a winter favorite. They can be easily made, and they make great gifts for parents or grandparents.

Materials for Each Child:

Baby food jar with a lid
Pinch of craft glitter
Small plastic ornament or cake decoration (a snowperson, a sleigh, or some other wintery thing)
Some silicon glue
Water

Procedure:

1. Carefully glue the ornament to the lid of the baby food jar. Allow to dry.

2. Fill the jar with water and add the pinch of glitter.

3. Run a bit of the silicon glue around the inside of the lid so that when it is screwed on, it will form a waterproof seal.

4. Store the snowglobe with the lid up overnight.

5. The next day, turn the snowglobe over and shake it.

Better Snowflakes
(a teacher-led activity)

Materials:

Two sheets of paper (white copier paper works great)
Stapler
Scissors

Procedure:

1. Staple or tape the two sheets together to make one long sheet. (*Time saver*: Use computer paper!) Beginning at the narrow edge, fold the paper accordion fashion. Make the folds about 1/2 inch wide until you have a narrow rectangle. (See Figure 1.)

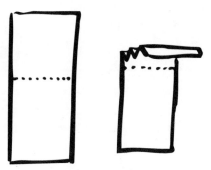

Figure 1

2. Cut the four corners of the rectangle at a diagonal. Then cut designs in both sides of the rectangles and put a staple in the center of the rectangle (See Figure 2.)

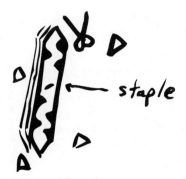

Figure 2

3. Open up the rectangle as you would a fan, top and bottom, and staple the edges together to form a circle. (See Figure 3.)

Figure 3

4. Adding gold glitter is fine, but the whole snowflake looks better if you wash the paper with light blue and pink watercolors and let dry before making the snowflake. When finished, hang the snowflakes from the light fixtures for a "really cool" classroom! (See Figure 4.)

Figure 4

Jumping into Spring

Seasonal themes are necessary for at least two reasons. First, the obvious changes from one season to the next make applying math and science concepts easy and natural. Second, in areas where winter is characterized by snow and cold, the coming Spring is welcome indeed.

One of the symbols of spring is the hatching chick. While nothing introduces a spring theme more profoundly than incubating fertilized chicken eggs, you can tap into the "hatching egg" idea in another way. It's less fascinating, perhaps, but it requires less time and technology.

Usually around Easter local department stores will have a supply of colorful plastic eggs that can be separated into halves and snapped back together. When you have these eggs in the classroom, write "springtime" notes or find "spring" pictures in magazines. Cut theses notes or pictures in half and put the halves in separate eggs. On the first nice day of spring, when children would rather be outside anyway, find a large outdoor area and disperse the colored plastic eggs. They don't need to be well-hidden, because you'll want to spend most of the time letting the children find the classmate with the other half of the picture or message.

Science makes a very natural sequel into the academic areas. One of the activity sheets included in this theme invites children to make comparisons and contrasts between life in winter and in spring. The underlying concept in every one of the seasonal themes is CHANGE. Explore changes in science, math, and the way of life of animals and people as the seasons change.

Bibliography

Asimov, I. *Why Do We Have Seasons?* **Milwaukee: G. Stevens, 1991 (24 pages).** Describes how the seasons affect people, animals, and nature. Beautiful illustrations.

Barklem, J. *Spring Story.* **New York: Philomel, 1980 (31 pages).** A community of field mice spends a spring day planning a surprise party for their friend Wilbert.

Berger, M. *Seasons.* **New York: Doubleday, 1990 (45 pages).** An especially good book for explaining to young children the causes of the changing seasons.

Clifton, L. *The Boy Who Didn't Believe in Spring.* **New York: Dutton, 1973 (32 pages).** Two city boys hear that spring is "just around the corner," so they set out to find it.

Dragonwagon, C. *Strawberry Dress Escape.* **New York: Scribner, 1975 (32 pages).** A little girl escapes from her boring classroom and into the wonders of spring in the country.

Emberly, M. *Welcome Back, Sun!* **Boston: Little, Brown & Co, 1993 (unpaged).** A Norwegian family tries to hurry the coming of spring.

Gerstein, M. *The Story of May.* **New York: Harper Collins, 1993 (unpaged).** May is on a journey to visit Father December. Along the way she meets all her siblings and cousins (the other months of the year).

Hines, A. *Come to the Meadow.* **New York: Clarion, 1984 (32 pages).** A little girl wants to share the wonders of her favorite meadow with her family, but no one seems interested until Granny makes a suggestion.

Johnson, C. *Will Spring Be Early or Will Spring Be Late?* **New York: Harper & Row, 1959 (48 pages).** The groundhog predicts an early spring, but he's been duped by an artificial flower.

Krauss, R. *The Happy Day.* **New York: Harper & Row, 1949 (unpaged).** It looks like spring is on its way when forest animals find a lone flower growing through the snow.

Lambert, D. *The Seasons.* **London: Franklin Watts, 1983 (32 pages).** A fact book about the seasons in an easy-to-read format with illustrations.

Lobel, A. *Frog and Toad Are Friends.* **New York: Harper & Row, 1970 (64 pages).** Five more stories of the two best friends. One is very appropriate to the theme; others will fit elsewhere.

Love, K. *April Showers.* **NY: Thomas Crowell, 1948 (46 pages).** A collection of rhymes and poems about the rain in spring.

McCauley, J. *Baby Birds and How They Grow.* **Washington, D.C.: National Geographic, 1983 (31 pages).** Text and pictures show mother birds caring for their young.

Miller, J. *Season on the Farm.* **Englewood Cliffs, NJ: Prentice Hall, 1986 (32 pages).** Easy-to-understand text and photographs explore the changing seasons on the farm.

Minarek, E. *It's Spring!* **New York: Greenwillow, 1989 (24 pages).** From the author of the Little Bear books comes Pit and Pat, two bunnies who celebrate the coming of spring by frolicking among the flowers.

Parker, N. *Bugs.* **New York: Scholastic, 1987 (unpaged)** In the spring the icky, crawly things come out. Who are they? How do they live? What good are they? Answers to these questions and more are found in this book.

Rockwell, A. *My Spring Robin.* **New York: Macmillan, 1989 (24 pages).** A child searching for the first robin of spring finds a host of spring animals and plants.

Rylant, C. *Henry and Mudge in Puddle Trouble.* **New York: Bradbury, 1987 (32 pages).** The second in the Henry and Mudge series. Henry and his dog delight in spring, frolicking in puddles and playing with the new kittens in the house next door.

Santry, L. *Spring.* **Mahwah, NJ: Troll, 1983 (32 pages).** The signs of spring portrayed in easy-to-read text and with beautiful photographs.

Saulnier, K. *Spring Is Green.* **Washington, D.C.: Gallaudet College Press, 1982 (52 pages).** An interesting look at the aesthetic and scientific changes of spring, in text and in signed English. Broadens children's awareness of concepts of spring, language and disabilities.

Soya, K. *A House of Leaves.* **New York: Philomel, 1986 (24 pages).** Sarah builds a shelter from the rain that she gladly shares with bugs and other creatures.

Tresselt, A. *Hi, Mr. Robin!* **New York: Lothrop, Lee and Shepard, 1950 (26 pages).** In the cold and gray days of early spring, the first robin helps a little boy discover the signs of the changing seasons.

Walker, C. *How New Plants Grow.* **Cleveland, OH: Modern Curriculum Press, 1990 (unpaged)** The title really says it all. A "must-have" for any theme about spring.

Watts, B. *Butterfly and Caterpillar.* **Morristown, NJ: Silver Burdett, 1985 (unpagged)** The metamorphosis of fuzzy, wormy things into beautiful, wingy things is explored in this illustrated book. The story is told with beautiful photographs.

Whyte, R. *The Flower That Finally Grew.* **New York: Crown, 1970 (27 pages).** Just as a watched pot never boils, a planted seed seems never to grow while a little boy watches and waits.

NAME_____

SPRINGTIME BOOKS I'VE READ

1. _____ Title
   _____ Author
2. _____ Title
   _____ Author
3. _____ Title
   _____ Author
4. _____ Title
   _____ Author
5. _____ Title
   _____ Author

© 1995 by The Center for Applied Research in Education

The Boy Who Didn't Believe in Spring
by
Lucille Clifton

NAME _____

Directions:

In the book *The Boy Who Didn't Believe in Spring*, there is a misunderstanding because of an *IDIOM*. "Spring is just around the corner" really means that it is coming soon, but the boys thought that it really was around the corner. Look at the idioms below and explain what they really mean.

1. It's raining cats and dogs. _____
   _____

2. He's just a little shrimp. _____
   _____

3. Spring really snuck up on us this year. _____
   _____

4. The river is overflowing with fish this year. _____
   _____

5. I feel like I'm in a rut. _____
   _____

Hi, Mr. Robin!
by
Alvin Tresselt

NAME _____

Directions:

Hi, Mr. Robin! explains some of the changes that you can see when the winter changes to spring. What are some ways you and your family make changes when spring comes?

WINTER	SPRING
Clothes _____	Clothes _____
_____	_____
_____	_____
House _____	House _____
_____	_____
_____	_____
Fun _____	Fun _____
_____	_____
_____	_____
Food _____	Food _____
_____	_____
_____	_____

Reading

A Poetry Lesson
(a teacher-led activity)

1. Prepare to Read

To help children prepare for the poem, read aloud the book *Spring Is Green* by Saulnier, *Spring* by Santry, or any other available book that describes the changes of spring.

As a group, create a web and discuss its branches. Use SPRING in the center, with PLANTS, ANIMALS, WEATHER, and PEOPLE on the branches.

2. Read the Poem

Poetry has several advantages. It is usually short, which allows for choral and repeated reading. Both these activities will strengthen sight-word familiarity and allow practice in clear fluent oral reading. It is a good idea to write the poem on chart paper or oaktag and leave it on display for a time so that it can be read again and again. You might want to post a new poem each week and make a ritual of reading it chorally each morning.

3. Respond to the Poem

Encourage discussion with the following questions:

- Which season do you like best? What is one thing that makes that season your favorite?

- Most poems have a "speaker," someone who might say the things that are said in the poem. What kind of person is the speaker in this poem? Why do you think so?

- The first line says, "I thought today would never come." What do you think is special about the day the speaker is talking about?

- Does grass blush? Why do you think the author used that word? (It's a metaphor, since spring is the season for love.)

The Best Thing About Spring
a poem by
Karl A. Matz

I thought today would never come
   But here it is at last.
      The sun is warm, the snow is gone,
         and birds are flying past.

The grass is blushing a yellowish green
   and the wise old owl hoots,
      "I think it's time to put away
         your sweaters, gloves, and boots."

Summer is fun and autumn is pretty
   But I like spring far more;
      For soon I'll run for the very last time
         Out through the schoolhouse door!

NAME_____

Spring Walks

Directions:
Think about your trip to school today. Use **saw** and **have seen** to write sentences about what you saw on your trip.

(SAW)_____

_____

_____

(HAVE SEEN)_____

_____

_____

(SAW)_____

_____

_____

(HAVE SEEN)_____

_____

_____

(SAW)_____

_____

_____

NAME _____

Lots of Action Going On!

Directions:

In the spring everything comes back to life. There is a LOT of action. Action words are called verbs. Circle the verbs below that show action.

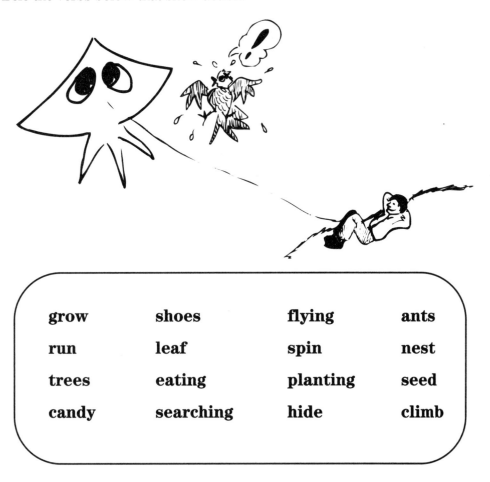

grow	shoes	flying	ants
run	leaf	spin	nest
trees	eating	planting	seed
candy	searching	hide	climb

Bonus:

Choose one of the verbs above and write a sentence about something you like to do on a warm spring day. _____

_____

_____

_____

Going on a Picnic
(a teacher-led activity)

A fun game that can be played anytime, "Going on a Picnic" is a great way to extend and encourage vocabulary.

Procedure:

Begin by saying, "I'm going on a picnic. Do you want to come with me? Then you must bring something for the picnic, too. It can be picnic supplies or food, but it must have a certain letter combination in its name. Who would like to come?"

As children begin guessing, you respond by saying, "Justin (child's name) may come with me" if Justin says a picnic word with the correct letter combination in its name or "Stacy may not come with me yet" if Stacy says a picnic word without the correct letter combination. As children guess the secret combination, they inform you by offering to bring something whose name has that combination, then they must keep it a secret. Reveal the secret before anyone shows frustration, then invite children in groups to take turns "Going on a Picnic."

Example:

Teacher:	"I'm going on a picnic. Do you want to come?"
Jeff:	"I'll bring the grapes!"
Teacher:	"Jeff may come with me!"
Sandy:	"I'll bring the oranges!"
Teacher:	"Sandy may come with me!"
Bill:	"I'll bring the basket!"
Teacher:	"Bill may not come with me yet!"

Soon the children will recognize that the secret combination requires a silent "e." They may begin to offer silverware, baseballs, tunes, etc.

Hydroponics
(a teacher-led activity)

Concepts:
Plants will grow in water without soil if the water is nutrient rich. Plants need light, water, and nutrients to grow. The nutrients are usually taken from the soil.

Materials:
Plant fertilizer (like Miracle-Gro)
Pea or bean seeds
Quart jar
Three small drinking glasses
Masking tape
Permanent marker
Some aluminum foil
A light source
Petri dish or saucer
Water

Procedure:
1. Germinate six seeds in the saucer with 5 mm of water. Add water as needed. First a root tip appears, then a shoot. Let the pea grow for about a week until the shoots are 5 mm long.
2. Choose the three healthiest plants.
3. Label the drinking glasses A, B, and C.
4. Mix a quart of plant fertilizer as directed in the quart jar.
5. Fill glass A and glass B half full with the solution. Use the masking tape to mark the level.
6. Fill glass C with only tap water (the control). Use the masking tape to mark the level.
7. Put all three glasses in bright sunlight and allow to grow. Add fertilizer solution or water as needed to replace the liquid that evaporates.
8. Observe the differences in growth among the three plants.

What Happens:
The plant in plain tap water will grow more slowly, and will have observably less green color than the plants in the nutrient solution.

NAME _____

How Are They Different?

Directions:

In many places there are some very important changes when winter turns to spring. Think of the world around January 1st and April 1st. What is different?

January 1	April 1
_____	_____
_____	_____
_____	_____
_____	_____
_____	_____
_____	_____
_____	_____
_____	_____
_____	_____
_____	_____
_____	_____
_____	_____

A Seasonal Terrarium
(a teacher-led activity)

Watch the changes of the seasons from Winter to Spring with a seasonal terrarium.

Materials:

Quart jars (use pint jars to complete the project on a smaller scale)
Potting soil
Varieties of seeds
Crushed ice

Procedure:

1. Lead a brainstorming discussion about the changes present as winter gives way to spring. This may be done as a follow-up to any one of the excellent books on the subject listed in the Bibliography.

2. Put the children in groups of four and provide each group with a jar.

3. The groups add potting soil to about 1/3 full.

4. Sprinkle seeds, then add another 1/4" of potting soil.

5. Add crushed ice to about 1" deep.

6. It is now Winter in the Seasonal Terrarium.

7. Put a lid on the terrarium and place it in a sunny window. The children should watch and, if you wish, journal the changes beginning with the melting snow which waters the tiny seeds. Within a few weeks, the warmth and moisture will encourage seedlings to creep cautiously upward. Eventually spring will come to the terrarium with tall, viable plants.

The Spring Equinox
(a teacher-led activity)

Concepts:

Observe the astronomical changes of spring.

Materials:

Metersticks
A sunny day
The weather report from today's newspaper

Procedure:

This activity is a follow-up to one of the science activities in the Autumn and Winter themes.

1. **Measure heights:** Find the permanent, erect object that was used in the autumn and winter measurements. Recall or measure its height. Do not use children's heights; they tend to grow and throw off subsequent measurements.

2. **Measure time:** Determine the exact "midday" by finding the time of sunrise and sunset, calculating the number of hours of daylight and dividing in half.

FOR EXAMPLE: If the sun rises at 7:15 and sets at 6:45, that's 11 hours and 30 minutes of daylight. Half that amount is 5 hours and 45 minutes. 7:15 plus 5:45 equals 13:00 or 1:00 p.m. (Older children can do this calculation themselves.)

3. **Measure lengths:** At exact midday, measure the length of the shadow cast by the object. Do not use a simple clock time (such as noon on September 21, December 21 and March 21) because daylight savings will cause gross inaccuracies.

4. Compare the length of the shadow taken in winter with the length of the shadow taken in spring. Younger children may stop here while older children continue with the geometry.

5. Compare the amount of daylight for the first days of autumn, winter, and spring and the time of each exact midday.

6. **Measure angles:** Older children may plot the angle of the sun by using graph paper to draw a scale model. The object forms one side of the angle, the shadow forms the base, and an imaginary line from the top of the object to the tip of the shadow forms the hypotenuse. Compare these angles for autumn, winter, and spring.

7. **Calculate ratios:** Find the ratio of object height to shadow length. FOR EXAMPLE: If the stop sign is 240 cm high and the shadow is 80 cm long, the "object to shadow ratio" is 240:80 or 3:1.

NAME _____

Basball Fun

Directions:

This is a card for a ball player named Iron Hand Jones. Look at the numbers on the back of the card and answer the questions below.

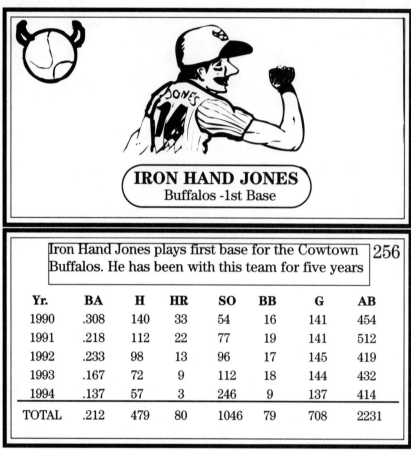

Iron Hand Jones plays first base for the Cowtown Buffalos. He has been with this team for five years — 256

Yr.	BA	H	HR	SO	BB	G	AB
1990	.308	140	33	54	16	141	454
1991	.218	112	22	77	19	141	512
1992	.233	98	13	96	17	145	419
1993	.167	72	9	112	18	144	432
1994	.137	57	3	246	9	137	414
TOTAL	.212	479	80	1046	79	708	2231

BA is BATTING AVERAGE   H is HITS   HR is HOMERUNS   SO is STRIKE OUTS
BB is WALKS (bases on balls)   G is GAMES   AB is AT BATS (number of times he batted)

1. During which year did Iron Hand get the most homers? _____
2. During what year did he get the least homers? _____
3. How many more times did he strike out in 1994 than in 1990? _____
4. A BA higher than 275 is good and lower than 225 is bad. Which years did Iron Hand have bad BA's? _____
5. Which years did he have good BA's? _____
6. Iron Hand was cut from the team in 1994. On the back of this page, explain why you think he was cut.

NAME _____

Spring Subtraction

Directions:

Use your subtraction skills to solve the following problems.

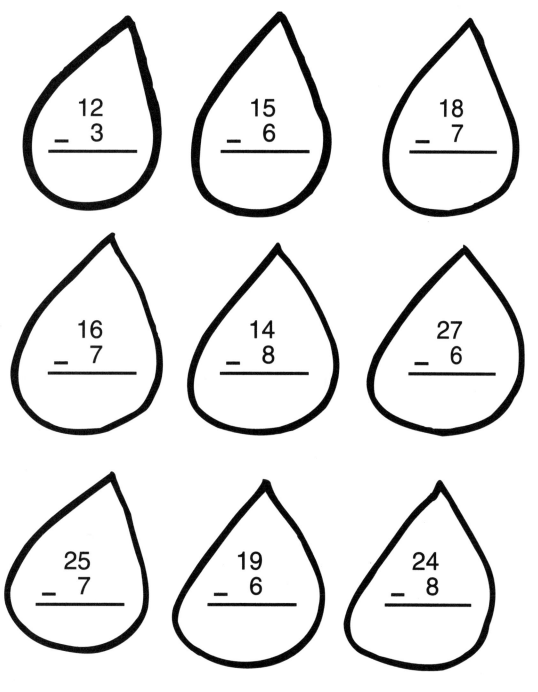

Where Did My Jacket Begin?
(a teacher-led activity)

Concepts:

A spring jacket is made of many different products. Many workers participate in making each jacket. Children will learn about the natural resources, manufacturing, and marketing of a jacket.

Procedure:

1. Obtain a common spring jacket and show it to the children. Invite them to name the various parts (lining, zipper, buttons) and what they are made of.

2. List these jacket parts and the materials they are made of on the board. Which materials are natural and which are made by people?

3. Where did the jacket owner get the jacket? (*store*) Where did the store get it? (*factory*) How did it get from the factory to the store? (*truck*) Follow the jacket in this way, backwards from the store to the origin of each part of the jacket. Use the accompanying worksheet for each student.

4. When the "journey" is finally described, list the many people who make their living creating materials, making the jacket, shipping it, and selling it.

5. Guide the children in filling out the sheet "Where Did My Jacket Begin?"

NAME _____

Where Did My Jacket Begin?

Materials	Material Makers

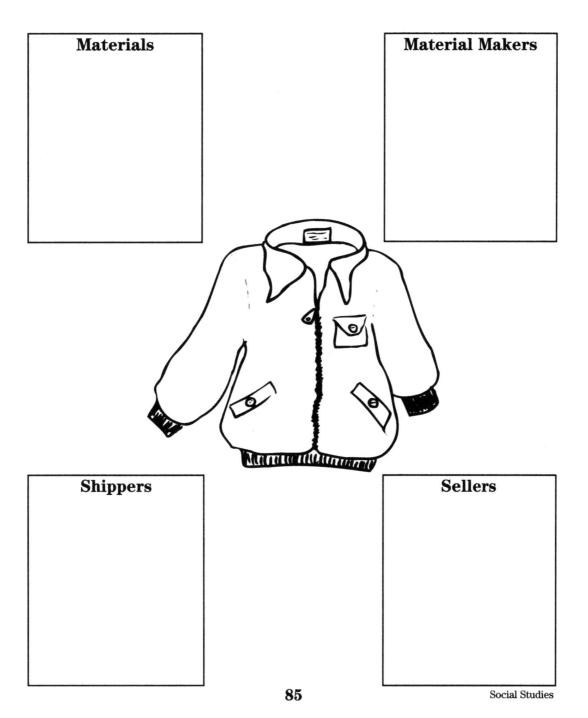

Shippers	Sellers

NAME_____

Vacation Time Is Almost Here!

Directions:

Spring is the time when many people begin to plan for summer vacations. Make a poster to invite them to visit your area. Choose one interesting place like a park, a river, or a famous building. Draw a picture and write a caption for it. Make your letters big and colorful.

© 1995 by The Center for Applied Research in Education

NAME_____

Welcome Spring

Directions:

In states where the winter is very long and cold, the spring is a welcome relief. Find the states that you think have cold winters and color them green. Look at a map and find the names of the states you colored. List them on the lines below.

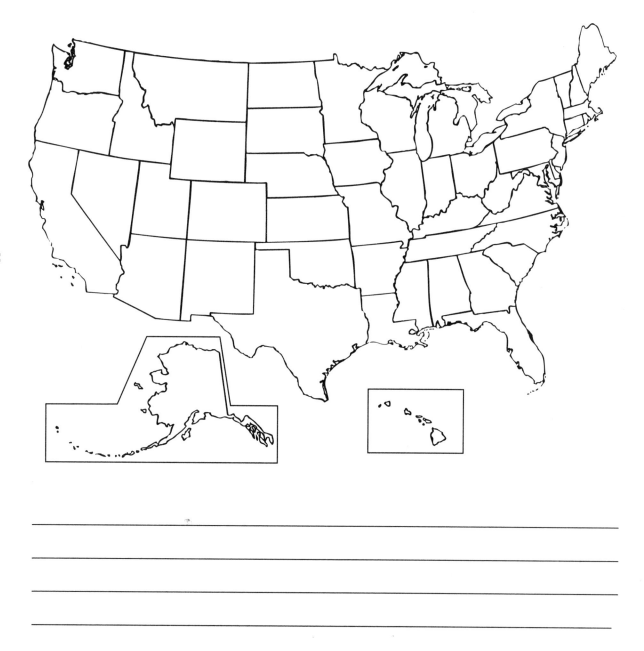

_____
_____
_____
_____

Magazine Butterflies
(a teacher-led activity)

Materials:

Brightly-colored, full-page pictures from magazines
Pipe cleaners
Small flat magnets like those used on refrigerator magnets
Templates (one set for every five or six children) made from
    Figures 1 and 2
Black or brown marker
Scissors
Tape

Procedure:

1. Trace the two template shapes onto the magazine photo.

2. Trace around the contours of the shapes again using a black or brown marker to make a 1/4" border.

3. Cut out the two shapes carefully, making sure to preserve the border you drew with your marker.

4. Pick up the square piece and "fan-fold," beginning at one corner and working diagonally to the opposite corner. Make your folds about 1/4" wide, trying to keep them uniform. This is the upper portion of the wings.

5. Pick up the lip-shaped piece and "fan-fold" as you did with the square, but horizontally from the bottom up. This is the bottom portion of the wings.

6. Hold the two wing portions between your thumb and index finger at the center.

7. Beginning at the center of the pipe cleaner, wrap once around. Let the two ends point upward and curl them into antennae.

8. Fluff out the two wing portions into brilliant and beautiful butterfly wings.

9. If you wish, a small magnet can be taped on the back and the butterflies can be displayed throughout the room. Another option is to make a mobile, by looping through the pipe strings at the top center.

Social Studies

Magazine Butterflies Templates

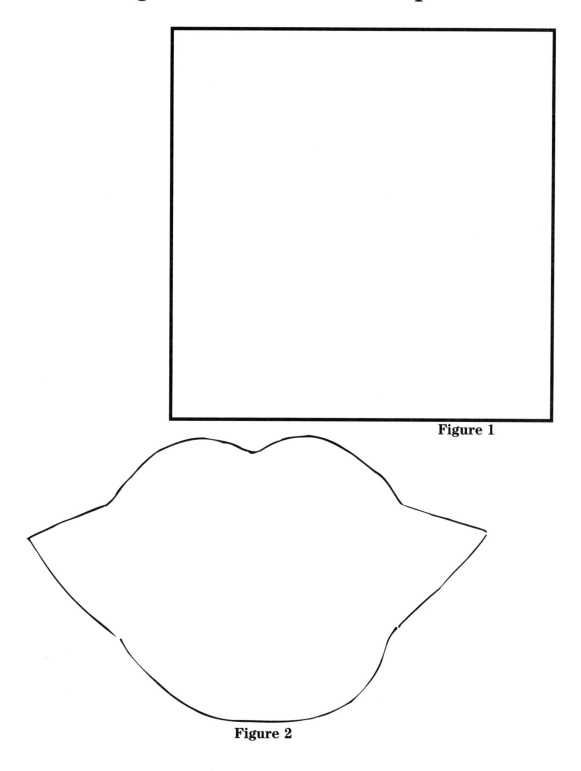

Figure 1

Figure 2

Summer

The End of the School Year

There comes a time in the late spring when children's hearts and minds are outside in the fresh green grass while their bodies are still in the same place they've been all winter. It's difficult to teach anything very demanding to a mind that is elsewhere, so most of us lighten the curriculum a bit with activities like field trips, plays, and puppet shows.

This difficulty is often the result of trying to bring the absent hearts back into the classroom. This theme is intended to do the opposite, to bring "school" to the place where the children are. If they are **thinking** about summer, then perhaps it would be a good time to **learn** about summer.

I like to pique their interest gradually. A bulletin board in the hall can be covered with bright yellow paper and in orange letters the simple promise:

It's Coming!

Leave that for a week or so and remain ambiguous when students ask for explanation. On Monday of the following week, place colorful cutouts of sunglasses at intervals in the hallway. On Wednesday add beachballs. On Friday add the colorful beach umbrellas. With every new item added to the halls, add one to the "It's Coming!" bulletin board.

A good way to start is with the lawn science activity in this theme. Children make faces on styrofoam cups, plant grass seed on the cups, and watch the funny faces grow hair! Later they will experiment with trimming and what happens when they don't!

Have fun with this theme, and enjoy a fun and relaxing summer!

Bulletin Board Idea

Bibliography

Allison, L. *The Sierra Club Summer Book.* **San Francisco: Sierra Club, 1977 (160 pages).** Great for science and art! Many excellent activities and useful facts about animals and the changes of summer.

Assiniboin Elders Board. *How the Summer Came.* **Washington, D.C.: National Institute of Education, 1981 (18 pages).** A retelling of a Native American legend of the coming of Summer. A government document with black-and-white illustrations.

Branley, F. *Sunshine Makes the Seasons.* **New York: Crowell, 1974 (33 pages).** Describes how the tilt of the Earth and the sunshine affect the weather and cause the changing seasons.

Brown, M. *D.W. All Wet.* **Boston: Joy Street, 1988 (22 pages).** One of the popular "Arthur books." D.W. hates the water and persuades Arthur to carry her around the beach on his shoulders.

Cooney, B. *Hattie and Wild Waves.* **New York: Viking, 1990 (38 pages).** A little girl from Brooklyn enjoys a summer at a beach where she listens to "the wild waves" and paints beautiful pictures.

Hirschi, R. *Summer.* **New York: Cobblehill, 1991 (unpaged).** Shows how baby animals born in spring spend the summer growing and learning.

Keller, H. *Henry's Fourth of July.* **New York: Greenwillow, 1985 (32 pages).** Henry and his family have a fun (and tiring!) day celebrating Independence Day.

Kimmelman, L. *Frannie's Fruits.* **New York: Harper & Row, 1989 (30 pages).** Frannie is a dog whose owners operate a fruit stand at the beach. Frannie helps — sometimes.

Lester, A. *Magic Beach.* **Boston: Joy Street, 1992 (unpaged).** Rhyming text and color illustrations bring to life the activities one can enjoy at the beach.

Lobel, A. *Alison's Zinnia.* **New York: Greenwillow, 1990 (unpaged).** An alphabet book that employs flowers such as amaryllis, begonia, carnation, etc.

Michels, T. *At the Frog Pond.* **New York: Lippincott, 1989 (32 pages).** Learn all about the variety of life in a pond from the cool spring days through the dog days of summer.

Milburn, C. *Let's Look at the Seasons.* **New York: Bookwright, 1988 (31 pages.)** From the "Let's Look At" series, this book describes the causes and effects of the changing seasons with simple language and colorful illustrations.

O'Donnell, E. *The Twelve Days of Summer.* **New York: Morrow, 1991. (unpaged).** A counting book. A little girl counts the things she sees at the beach on a summer day.

Polgren, J. *Sunlight and Shadows.* **New York: Doubleday, 1967 (57 pages).** Explains why shadows exist and how they are affected by the changing seasons.

Regan, D. *The Class With the Summer Birthdays.* **New York: Holt, 1991 (74 pages).** A third-grade class has a birthday party for all the children born in summer. A great activity for any class's summer theme.

Santry, L. *Summer.* **Mahwah, NJ: Troll, 1983 (32 pages).** From the "Discover the Seasons" series. Easy-to-understand text and colorful photographs explore the changes in weather, plant growth, and animal behavior that occur in summer.

Schweninger, A. *Summertime.* **New York: Viking, 1992 (unpaged).** The changes from spring to summer are discussed in this book.

Selberg, I. *Our Changing World.* **New York: Philomel, 1982 (13 pages).** A picture book that depicts the changing seasons in various habitats such as mountains, lakes, woods, desert, and frozen tundra.

Sis, P. *Beach Ball.* **New York: Greenwillow, 1990 (26 pages).** Mostly colored illustrations and simple text teach numbers, colors, shapes, and letters in the context of a little girl and her mother visiting the beach.

Webster, D. *Exploring Nature Around the Year: Summer.* **Englewood Cliffs, NJ: J. Messner, 1990 (48 pages).** Filled with activities and projects, this book will help children explore nature in summer.

Zappler, G. *Science in Summer and Fall.* **Garden City, NY: Doubleday, 1974 (177 pages).** Though difficult for young children, this book may prove to be an indispensible teacher resource. Many interesting and easy activities.

SUMMER BOOKS I'VE READ

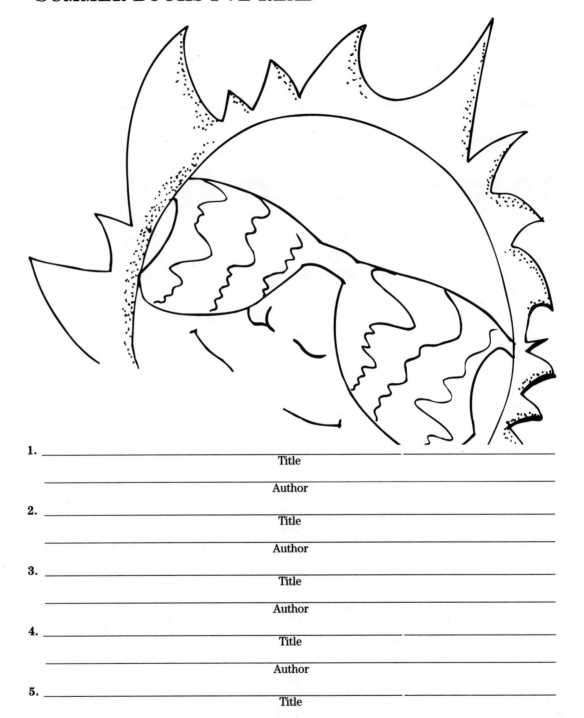

1. _____
   Title
   _____
   Author
2. _____
   Title
   _____
   Author
3. _____
   Title
   _____
   Author
4. _____
   Title
   _____
   Author
5. _____
   Title
   _____
   Author

NAME _____

A Summer Day
by
Douglas Florian

NAME _____

Directions:

Plan a picnic!

1. Who will you invite? _____
   _____
   _____

2. What foods will you bring along? _____
   _____
   _____

3. Where will you go to have the picnic? _____
   _____

4. What can you do there for fun before and after you eat? _____
   _____
   _____

5. What day could you go? _____

6. How will you get yourself and your friends to the picnic? _____
   _____
   _____

The Sun's Asleep Behind the Hill
by Mirra Ginsberg

NAME _____

Directions:

On the lines below, describe how you and your family get ready to sleep.

_____
_____
_____
_____
_____
_____
_____
_____
_____
_____
_____
_____

**Basil Brush
at the Beach**
by Peter Firmin

NAME _____

Directions:

Basil and Harry are angry with each other after their day at the beach. Write a note to them to help them become friends again.

Dear Basil and Harry,

Compounds

Directions:

Use the words below to make compound summer words. Each word may be used more than once.

ball	sun	moon	house	rain	rise
camp	bath	fall	light	out	set
dug	base	foot	fire	dog	glow
bird	path				coat

NAME _____

What's the Question?

Directions:

Here are some answers about summer, but I lost the questions. Can you help me? Write a good question for each answer. Use complete sentences.

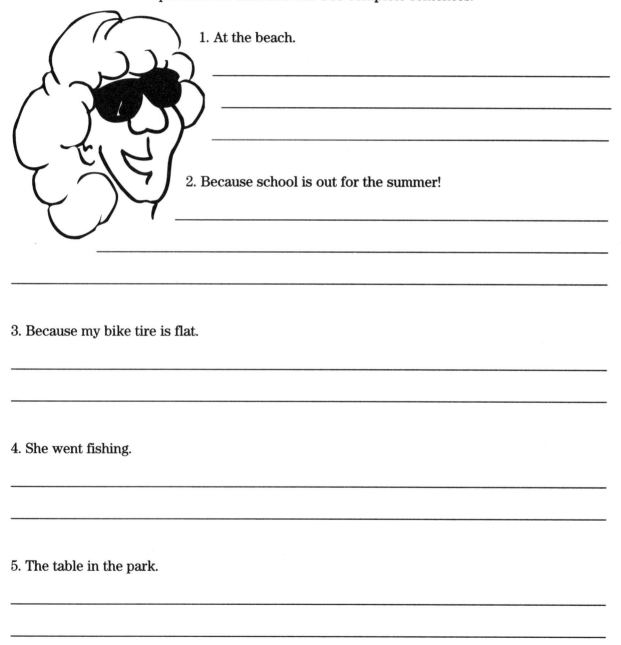

1. At the beach.

_____
_____
_____

2. Because school is out for the summer!

_____
_____

3. Because my bike tire is flat.

_____
_____

4. She went fishing.

_____
_____

5. The table in the park.

_____
_____

NAME _____

Fact or Opinion

Directions:

A fact is something that's always true no matter what anyone thinks. An opinion is something some people believe but other people don't. Read the sentences below. Circle **FACT** if the sentence is always true or **OPINION** if the sentence is just something some people believe.

1. Summer is the best time of year.   **FACT**   **OPINION**

2. The sun sets later in the summer.   **FACT**   **OPINION**

3. Bluebirds are very pretty.   **FACT**   **OPINION**

4. Baseball is the very best game of all!   **FACT**   **OPINION**

5. Summer starts on June 21.   **FACT**   **OPINION**

6. Many people visit Mount Rushmore in the summer.   **FACT**   **OPINION**

7. Mount Rushmore is the prettiest thing in the world.   **FACT**   **OPINION**

8. Bike riding is more fun than swimming!   **FACT**   **OPINION**

9. Our teacher is the best teacher in the world.   **FACT**   **OPINION**

10. This is the last sentence on this page.   **FACT**   **OPINION**

Leaf Cuttings
(a teacher-led activity)

Plants grow from many different plant parts including seeds, bulbs, shoots, stems, and leaves. Many elementary children are unaware of this, thinking instead that plants grow only from seeds. This activity will broaden their experience and understanding.

Materials:
African violets
Potting soil
Large plastic drinking cups
Plastic storage bags

Procedure:

1. Divide the class into groups of four.

2. Begin by asking the children to tell where plants come from. Facilitate by questioning until their collective knowledge is exhausted. Continue by introducing this activity.

3. Give each group a drinking cup about 3/4 filled with potting soil.

4. Each group should lightly water until the soil is moist, but not saturated.

5. Each group receives two leaves, with stems intact, freshly cut from the violet.

6. Carefully transplant the leaf cuttings into the soil.

7. Place the pot in the storage bag and seal. This will serve as a greenhouse.

8. Place the pot in a warm place with plenty of sunlight.

9. Within a couple of weeks, tiny plants should appear around the base of the leaf cutting.

10. Explain that not all leaves will grow new plants. Only certain plants have this characteristic, just as only certain animals can fly or swim or run.

A Sundial
(a teacher-led activity)

Sundials are an ancient way to use the sun to measure time. The activity below integrates social studies, math, and science concepts very naturally.

Materials:
One-foot square of stiff white paper or oaktag
One-foot diameter circle template to trace
One-foot squares of corrugated cardboard
Eight-inch dowels or new pencils
Ruler
Glue

Procedure:

1. Offer this premise: "Imagine we lived in the time of Kings and Queens. There is no electricity or machinery. What are some ways we could tell time?" Encourage brainstorming.
2. Explain to children that long ago, before electronics and machinery, people still needed a way to measure time. They marked the passing of time by measuring the changes in shadows.
3. Arrange the class into groups of four.
4. Provide each group with a white square, a cardboard square, a circle template, and a dowel.
5. Use a ruler to draw an X from corner to corner across the middle of the white square. This will allow you to find the center.
6. Use the template to trace a circle on the white paper.
7. Glue the white paper to the corrugated cardboard to make it more sturdy.
8. Make a neat hole in the exact center of the X. Insert and secure the dowel.
9. Put the sundial in a safe sunny place. At ten o'clock on a sunny day, trace the shadow cast by the dowel and label this 10. Repeat at noon and label with 12. Repeat again at two o'clock and label with 2. When these are in place the hours of 11 and 1 can be added by measuring.
10. The children may notice as the days pass and summer draws nearer that the sundial becomes less accurate. This may be an appropriate time to explain how hours of daylight increase and decrease with passing seasons.

Lawn Science
(a teacher-led activity)

Concepts:
We see lawns everyday, but there is interesting science in observing how it grows.

Materials:
Small styrofoam cups
Potting soil
Construction paper
Grass seed
Scissors

Procedure:

1. Use construction paper to make faces on the styrofoam cups. Try to make them funny because when the grass grows it will complete the face with a shaggy head of green "hair."
2. Place potting soil in the container, sow the seed, and water it. Place it in a sunny window.
3. Let the seed grow, watering as needed.
4. Observe each day and measure the blades. Record observations or take pictures every other day.
5. When the grass is about 4 cm long, trim half the plot back to 5 mm and allow the other half to continue growing. (Give it a hair cut.)
6. Allow the long grass to go to seed. Observe and record this process.

What happens: Grass seed grows from its base and will continue growing when trimmed. If allowed to do so, it will grow quite tall and eventually "go to seed."

 NAME _____

Fill in the Thermometer

Directions:
The person who made this thermometer forgot some of the numbers. See if you can finish the job.

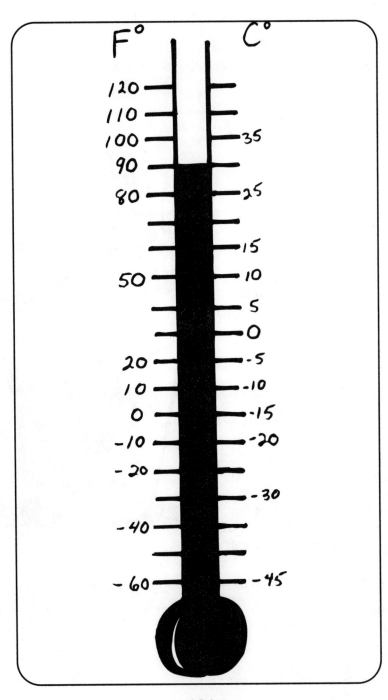

A Summer Friend

Directions:

Solve the problems below, then color the spaces with the answers to find a summer friend.

```
  60        26        35        18
 +17       +23       +44       +13

  32        41        53        26
 +55       +28       +45       +62

  23        44        41        26
 +60       +18       +13       +17

  23        32        35        60
 +17       +21       +51       +16
```

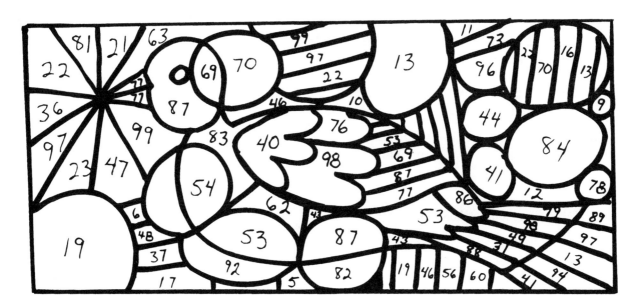

 NAME _____

Ice Cream—Yummy!

Directions:

You are working on the ice cream truck this summer. Use your arithmetic skills to help the customers below.

The Tasty Iceman

Lemon ice	25 cents per scoop
Ice cream bars	75 cents each
Chocolate-covered bananas	50 cents each
Milkshakes	90 cents each
Banana splits	30 cents per scoop
Fudgebars	50 cents each
Frozen pops	30 cents each
Lemonade	60 cents a cup

How much will it cost?

1. I'd like two scoops of lemon ice in a dish and a cup of lemonade. _____

2. I want two milkshakes and one frozen pop. _____

3. Could I have a chocolate-covered banana and two ice cream bars? _____

4. Ummmmm. I'll take a banana split with three scoops. _____

5. My turn? Okay, I'll have a milkshake, a fudgebar, and one scoop of lemon ice. _____

Bonus: **Bonus:**

6. What can I get for 50 cents? _____
   _____
   _____

© 1995 by The Center for Applied Research in Education

Vacation Travel Guides
(a teacher-led activity)

Concepts:

In the summer, many people travel to other places to see the interesting and educational sites they have to offer. How do they decide where to go? Many people send for guidebooks and pamphlets from travel agencies and departments of tourism.

Materials:

Art and drawing paper
Examples of travel pamphlets
Art materials as needed
Copies of the QUAD worksheet

Procedure:

1. **Brainstorm:** What interesting places in our area should people come to see this summer? List all reasonable responses on the board or overhead.

2. **Study the models:** Look at pamphlets to see what information they include. (*Subtopics:* How to get there, what to bring, background information, where to stay, where to eat, pictures of the attraction or event.)

3. **Groups:** Divide into groups of six. Each group will create a pamphlet about one attraction or event. *Roles:* editor, research assistants, and layout and graphic artists. The editor is responsible for the coordination of the final product, will arrange typing, and oversee layout. Research assistants gather information and write short, interesting paragraphs about specific subtopics.

4. **QUAD:** The QUAD (Question, Answer, Detail) worksheet helps groups arrange the needed content.

5. **Research and Writing:** Research assistants go forth with assignments and gather information that answer questions on the QUAD.

6. **Illustration and Layout:** When all the information is gathered and written, it is typed (30 characters per line for a pamphlet, or more if smaller type is used). Text and pictures are cut and pasted to make an attractive, organized pamphlet.

7. **Final product:** The pamphlets can be displayed in the classroom's "Department of Vacations" or in the school's library, main lobby or foyer. Make posters, such as "Plan a Great Vacation in Your Own Home Town" or something similar and display pamphlets that encourage visitors to see your area.

Q U A D
(QUESTION, ANSWER, DETAIL)

QUESTIONS	ANSWERS	DETAILS
1. Name of the place or event.		
2. History of it.		
3. How do people get there?		
4. What other interesting places are nearby?		
5. Where are the nearest places to eat?		
6. Where are the nearest hotels?		

Summer on Cleo's Island
by Natalie G. Sylvester

NAME _____

Directions:

This book contains a map of the island Cleo's family visits each summer. Draw a map of your neighborhood. Label the places to which you often go.

Summer

Let's Fly a Kite
(a teacher-led activity)

Although kite flying is usually considered a springtime activity, the end of the school year is a perfect time for making and flying them.

The classic "Eddy bow" kite is all but forgotten in this age of vinyl and plastic, but the style is still workable and easy to make and adorn. You will need (for each group of 4 children) two sticks of thin pine or balsa wood (approximately 36" long x 1/4" x 1/8" in thickness), a ball of kite string, lightweight butcher paper, glue, masking tape, and cloth scraps.

Procedure:

1. Using a coping saw or jigsaw, slot each end of the sticks to a depth of about 1/16" to accommodate the string frame. (See Figure 1.)

   Figure 1

2. Choose one stick to be the cross-piece. Mark the center. On the other stick, mark a point about 6 inches from one end. Fasten the sticks into a cross at the marked points. (See Figure 2.)

   Figure 2

3. Frame the cross with string. Slip it into the slot and wrap it twice. (See Figure 3.)

   Figure 3

4. Cut a sheet of butcher paper that is slightly larger (by 2 inches all around) than the framed cross you've created. Miter the corners so that the ends of the sticks will show and the paper will not overlap. (See Figure 4.)

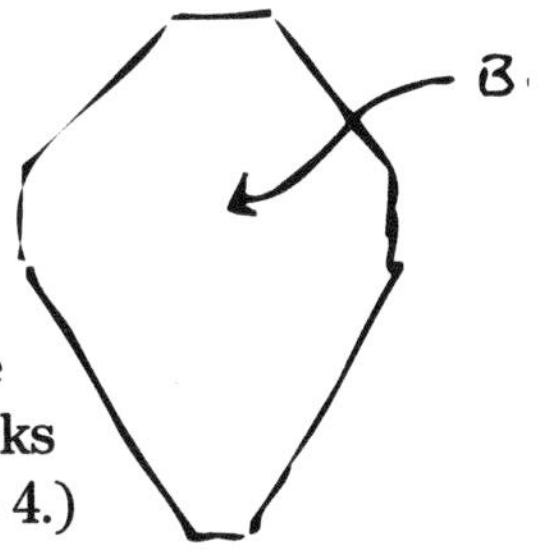

   Figure 4

5. Express yourself artistically with markers, crayons, or paint. (See Figure 5.)

6. Lay the paper face-down on a flat surface. Lay the framed cross down on top. Fold the edges over and glue them down with white glue. Allow to dry overnight. (See Figure 6.)

Figure 5

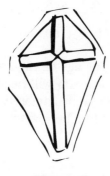

Figure 6

7. Put a square of masking tape on the front of the kite at 4 inches from each end to reinforce the bridal. Very gently, make holes through the masking tape patches. Carefully notch the vertical stick at the point where the holes were made. Run one end of a string through the top hole and tie firmly to the vertical stick at the notch. Run the string through the bottom hole and affix to the vertical stick. Leave enough slack in the bridal string so that it can be held away from the kite 8 to 12 inches. (See Figure 7.)

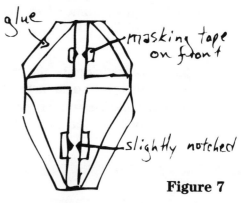

Figure 7

8. With another piece of string, form a shallow bow with the cross stick. Tie one end of the string firmly to one end of the horizontal stick. Bend the stick slightly to form a bow and firmly fix the string to the other end of the stick. (See Figure 8.)

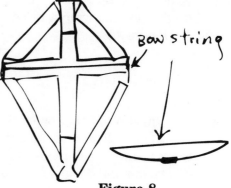

Figure 8

9. Tie the kite string to the bridal string so that it slides up and down the bridal fairly easily. This will allow the kite to adjust to the natural force of the wind. (See Figure 9.)

10. Most Eddy bow kites need some kind of tail. Cut a length of kite string equal to 1-1/2 times the length of the kite and affix to the bottom of the vertical stick. Tie scraps of cloth to the string at intervals of 4 to 8 inches. The tail keeps the kite upright as it flies.

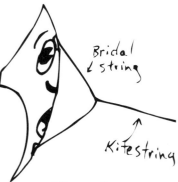

Figure 9

11. To fly the kite, you will need a day with winds of 10 to 12 miles per hour. Be sure you have plenty of room to stay clear of power lines, trees, and buildings. Have one person hold the string with his or her back to the wind while the other carries the kite out about 30 yards. When the wind takes the kite upward, the holder should let go. Controlling a kite in the air takes a little practice. (See Figure 10.)

Figure 10

The Family

A Theme for All Seasons

While a study of the family has always been part of the school curriculum in social studies, the diversity of families of today makes it all the more important. It's not merely a unit for giving primary children "warm fuzzies" anymore; it is a study of society and culture. The materials provided in this theme seek to broaden children's awareness of how different people think of families, how human families differ from animal families, and how families get along financially.

A good way to enter the theme is with a classic survey and graphing activity. Be sure the bulletin board is displayed, because the ambiance of the room will always add to the feeling that we are embarking on something new and novel. Write the numbers 2 through 15 on the board and draw a straight line above them, like so:

---

2   3   4   5   6   7   8   9   10   11   12   13   14   15

Give each child a self-stick note and have them write their names on it. Invite children to come up one at a time and place a self-stick note carefully above the number that represents the number in their family (adult and child).

When each child has entered his or her data on the graph, pose these questions:

1. What family size do most of us have?

2. What family size do the least of us have?

3. How many more people are in the biggest family compared to the smallest?

Ask children to take out a sheet of paper and fold it in half "the long way." On the left they should write the heading ADVANTAGES and on the right DISADVANTAGES. Have children think about living in a family of 16 children with 8 boys and 8 girls. What would be the advantages? What would be the disadvantages? Repeat with the premise, "You're an only child." What are the advantages and disadvantages? Follow up by reading *Alexander and the Terrible, Horrible, No Good Very Bad Day*.

The Family Bibliography

Ackerman K. *The Song and Dance Man.* **New York: Scholastic, 1988 (28 pages).** Grandpa was a song and dance man in vaudeville many years ago. These days he is content doing his act when his grandchildren come to visit.

Arnstein, H. S. *Billy and Our New Baby.* **New York: Behavioral Publications, 1973 (35 pages).** Billy is jealous of the new baby so he tries to act like a baby to get his family's attention. He soon learns he likes being a big boy much better.

Bonsall, C. *The Day I Had to Play With My Sister.* **New York: Harper & Row, 1972 (32 pages).** A little boy is frustrated while trying to teach his younger sister to play hide-and-seek.

Bronin, A. *Gus and Buster Work Things Out.* **New York: Dell, 1975 (61 pages).** Four stories of two brothers who, like most brothers, have moments of conflict and moments of love.

Brown, M. *D.W. All Wet.* **Boston: Joy Street Books, 1988 (22 pages)** D.W. nags her brother into carrying her on his shoulders at the beach. She hates the water, until Arthur provides her with a big surprise.

Bunting, E. *The Wednesday Surprise.* **New York: Clarion, 1989 (32 pages).** Anna and her grandmother share a special secret about what they do every Wednesday night. Won't Anna's Daddy be surprised when he learns that Anna taught Granny to read.

Caines, J. *Abby.* **New York: Harper & Row, 1984 (32 pages).** Abby is an adopted member of a very special family.

Carey, V. S. *Harriet and William and the Terrible Creature.* **New York: Dutton, 1985 (27 pages).** Twins who prefer to stay at home take a trip into outer space to help an unhappy dragon.

Delton, J. *Backyard Angel.* **Boston: Houghton-Mifflin, 1983. (107 pages).** Angel loves her little brother but being responsible for caring for him is almost more than she can bear.

Doss, H. *A Brother the Size of Me.* **Boston: Little, Brown & Co, 1957 (unpaged).** How could a child feel lonely in a family with six adopted children? Donny does and he wishes with all his heart for a brother his size to play with.

Edelman, E. *I Love My Baby Sister (Most of the Time)*. **New York: Lothrop & Lee, 1984 (32 pages).** Having a baby sister is not all fun and games, but one can always hope for a not-too-distant day when she will be old enough to play with.

Ehrlich, A. *Bunnies on Their Own*. **New York: Dial Books for Young Readers, 1986 (23 pages).** Mother bunny decides the children are old enough to be left on their own, but sister plays while brother does all the work.

Friedrich, A. *The Castles of the Two Brothers*. **New York: Holt, Rinehart & Winston, 1972 (40 pages).** Although he tries, Kalus can't get out from under the watchful eye of his older brother.

Gelman, R. G. *Dumb Joey*. **New York: Holt, Rinehart & Winston, 1973 (55 pages).** Joey's older brother considers him to be a pain, but one day Joey proves he can be useful.

Greenfield, E. *Grandpa's Face*. **New York: Putnam & Gossett, 1988 (30 pages).** Grandpa has a wonderful face, but one day Tamika sees an expression that scares her. Is Grandpa only acting?

Guilfoile, E. *Have You Seen My Brother?* **Chicago: Follette, 1962 (29 pages).** Andrew's brother is lost and Andrew is looking everywhere for him.

Hoban, R. *Harvey's Hideout*. **New York: Parents Magazine Press, 1969 (42 pages).** Harvey thinks his sister is mean and she thinks he is stupid. After several lonely hours playing apart, they rethink their positions.

Hooker, R. *At Grandma and Grandpa's House*. **Middletown, CT: Weekly Reader Books, 1986 (28 pages).** The joys and delights of a visit to Grandma and Grandpa's house. Children from the city find animals and birds, long hallways, games and toys, and soft comfy beds.

Hughes, S. *The Big Alfie and Annie Rose Storybook*. **New York: Lothrop, Lee & Shepard, 1988 (58 pages).** The adventures of young Alfie and his younger sister Annie.

Johnston, T. *Yonder*. **New York: Dial Books for Young Readers, 1988 (30 pages).** A beautiful story that follows a family through the seasons and across many years.

Miles, M. *Annie and the Old One*. **Boston: Joy Street, 1971 (44 pages).** A classic and award-winning story of a young Navajo girl and her desperate attempts to prevent her grandmother's passing.

Milgram, M. *Brothers Are All the Same*. **New York: Dutton, 1978 (32 pages).** No matter how they become members of the family, brothers and sisters are all the same.

Parish, P. *Amelia Bedelia's Family Album.* New York: Greenwillow Books, 1988 (48 pages). Amelia, always confused and confusing, shares her family album with the Rogerses and describes her relatives and what they do.

Pelligrini, N. *Families Are Different.* New York: Holiday House, 1991 (unpaged). A Korean girl adopted by an American family discovers that her classmates come from many different kinds of families.

Ringold, F. *Aunt Harriet's Underground Railroad in the Sky.* New York: Crown, 1993 (32 pages) Cassie is reunited with her brother by retracing the path of the Underground Railroad.

Rylant, C. *The Relatives Came.* New York: Bradbury Press, 1985 (28 pages). When the relatives come visiting from Virginia, everyone has a fun time!

Rylant, C. *When I Was Young in the Mountains.* New York: Bradbury Press, 1986 (28 pages). A host of recollections about life in the Appalachian mountains in days gone by.

Segal, L. G. *Tell Me a Mitzi.* New York: Farrar, Straus and Giroux, 1970 (40 pages). Three family stories in the life of a child called Mitzi: a trip to visit Grandma, a family cold, and an adventure with the President's motorcade.

Seligman, D. *Run Away Home.* San Carlos, CA: Golden Gate Junior Books, 1969 (31 pages). During one day when everything seems to go wrong, young Billy runs away from home.

Sharmat, Marjorie. *The Day I Was Born.* New York: Dutton, 1980 (30 pages). A boy recounts for his younger brother the story of the day of his birth.

Sharmat, Marjorie. *A Big Fat Enormous Lie.* New York: Dutton, 1978 (28 pages). A boy tells a lie to his parents, and that big green lie with its runny nose follows him around, getting bigger and bigger until he finds a way to tell the truth.

Sharmat, Mitchell. *Gregory, the Terrible Eater.* New York: Scholastic, 1980 (28 pages). Gregory is a goat who refuses to eat cans and waste paper. His parents are frustrated because all he wants to eat are balanced meals.

Shyer, M. *Here I Am an Only Child.* New York: Scribners, 1985 (unpaged). Being an only child has its ups and downs. Both are explored in this charmingly illustrated treasure.

Sonneborn, R. *Friday Night Is Papa Night.* New York: Viking Press, 1970 (31 pages). Papa is gone all week and comes home on Friday nights, but this week Papa doesn't show. Is something wrong?

Viorst, J. *The Goodbye Book.* **New York: Macmillan, 1988 (29 pages).** little boy tries to keep his parents from going out, but he gets a surprise when the babysitter arrives.

Viorst, J. *I'll Fix Anthony.* **New York: Harper & Row, 1989 (32 pages).** A little brother tells of his dreams of someday doing all sorts of things better than his big brother Anthony.

Walton, S. *Books Are for Eating.* **New York: Dutton, 1989 (24 pages).** Katy is appalled by the new baby's behavior and is absolutely certain that she never acted so badly when she was a baby.

Wells, R. *Don't Spill It Again!* **New York: Dial Press, 1977 (48 pages).** Three stories about James and his bossy but loveable older brother.

Williams, V. *A Chair for My Mother.* **New York: Greenwillow Books, 1982 (32 pages).** A child, her mother and grandmother save dimes to buy a chair after all their furniture is lost in a fire.

Yardley, J. *The Red Ball.* **San Diego: Harcourt Brace Jovanovich, 1991 (unpaged).** A magic red ball leads a little girl to some family photographs of some people who remind her of herself.

Zolotow, C. *Big Sister, Little Sister.* **New York: Harper, 1966 (28 pages).** When a little sister runs away, she finds out just how much her bossy big sister really cares.

Zolotow, C. *Do You Know What I'll Do?* **New York: Harper & Row, 1958 (27 pages).** One of America's best-loved authors wrote this classic about a little girl and her baby brother.

NAME_____

BOOKS I'VE READ ABOUT FAMILIES

1. _____
   Title
   _____
   Author

2. _____
   Title
   _____
   Author

3. _____
   Title
   _____
   Author

4. _____
   Title
   _____
   Author

© 1995 by The Center for Applied Research in Education

The Wednesday Surprise
by Eve Bunting

NAME _____

Directions:

Think about how Anna's Grandma did things before Anna taught her to read. Write your ideas below.

Grandma would not be able to read the directions to put a new toy together. NAME FIVE MORE THINGS SHE COULD NOT DO.

1. _____
2. _____
3. _____
4. _____
5. _____

Choose one of your ideas above and try to think of ways that Grandma might do it without reading. (Maybe she could look at the pictures to help her put together a new toy.)

_____
_____
_____
_____
_____
_____

Reading

All Kinds of Families
by
Norma Simon

NAME_____

Directions:
Families get together for holidays, weddings, birthdays, and other celebrations. Sometimes families have huge family reunions. Have you been to a family celebration? Tell about it. Use complete sentences.

1. What kind of get-together was it?
_____
_____

2. When did it happen?
_____
_____

3. Where was it held?
_____
_____

4. How did you get there and how long did it take?
_____
_____

5. Who else was there in addition to the family that lives in your house?
_____
_____

6. What was the best part?
_____
_____

7. What was one thing you didn't like much?
_____
_____

> **Yonder**
> by
> Tony Johnston

NAME _____

Directions:

In *Yonder*, Tony Johnston tells the story of a family through many seasons and across many years. Find out all you can from your parents and grandparents about the first people from your family that came to your state or your town. Find out how your family ended up where it did.

1. The first member of my family to come to America was _____

   _____ in the year _____ from the country

   of _____. That person lived in

   _____ after coming to America.

2. My grandma grew up in_____.

3. My grandpa grew up in_____.

4. My other grandma grew up in_____.

5. My other grandpa grew up in_____.

6. My mom grew up in_____.

7. My dad grew up in_____.

8. I now live in_____.

The Family

NAME _____

Describe the Relationships

Directions:

Use the lines below to describe the relationships between the family members in the stories. Be sure to use complete sentences.

Little Red Riding Hood

_____
_____
_____
_____

Cinderella

_____
_____
_____
_____

Jack and the Beanstalk

_____
_____
_____
_____

© 1995 by The Center for Applied Research in Education

The Family

NAME _____

Family Facts

Directions:
The sentences below are answers to questions about your family. Your job is to write the questions.

1. **The answer is** . . . Every Saturday morning.

The question is _____

_____

2. **The answer is** . . . Only during holidays.

The question is _____

_____

3. **The answer is** . . . Because everyone in my family likes it.

The question is _____

_____

4. **The answer is** . . . Because it is too far away.

The question is _____

_____

5. **The answer is** . . . If we didn't, someone in the family would be sad.

The question is _____

_____

The Family

NAME _____

A Writing Activity

Directions:
Use this sheet to help you write a page for your class book "When I was young in . . ."

When I was young in _____, my friends

and I would _____

_____.

When I was young in _____,

my mother would _____

_____.

When I was young in _____,

my favorite season was _____

because _____

_____

_____

© 1995 by The Center for Applied Research in Education

Language Arts

The Family

NAME _____

Your Heredity

Directions:

We all take after our mothers, fathers, and grandparents. This is called "heredity." Fill out the tables below about your parents and yourself. Answer the questions that follow to find your own heredity.

YOU

Eye color _____

Hair color _____

Hair type (straight curly wavy)

Skin (light medium dark freckles)

YOUR MOM

Eye color _____

Hair color _____

Hair type (straight curly wavy)

Skin (light medium dark freckles)

YOUR DAD

Eye color _____

Hair color _____

Hair type (straight curly wavy)

Skin (light medium dark freckles)

---

1. Whose eye color did you inherit? _____

2. Whose hair color did you inherit? _____

3. Whose hair type did you inherit? _____

4. Whose skin color did you inherit? _____

5. Can you think of one more thing you got from one of your parents (think of nose, eyebrows, chin, and others)? _____

The Family

NAME _____

Animals as Parents

Directions:

Some animals are very good parents. Others are not. Find out about the animals below and answer the three questions about each.

Animal Name	What does the family live in?	Does the mother feed the babies?	Does the father help out?
ROBIN			
TIGER			
SALMON			
CAT			
GOOSE			
BEAR			
WOLF			

The Family

NAME _____

The Alvarez Family

Directions:

Use your math skills to solve the story problems below. Turn this page over to work out the problems. Be sure to decide which sign to use.

1. The Alvarez family has 11 people in it. Every week they spend $212.00 on groceries. How much do they spend on groceries each year?

2. Mrs. Alvarez works for the Bansing Computer Co. She makes $16.50 per hour. If she works 40 hours each week, how much will she make per week?

3. Everyone in the Alvarez family drinks an 8-ounce glass of orange juice each morning. How many ounces of orange juice does the family drink each day?

4. How much does the family drink each week?

5. How much does the family drink each month?

6. Below are the ages of the children. Put them in order from oldest to youngest.

Name	Age
Sandy	5
Arnold	11
Glenn	2
Connie	7
Rhonda	13
Fanny	9
Ernesto	15
Hazel	17
Stan	1

Name	Age
_____	____
_____	____
_____	____
_____	____
_____	____
_____	____
_____	____
_____	____
_____	____

The Family

The Alvarez Family's Grocery Bill

Directions:

The Alvarez family is trying to save money. They usually shop at Northwest Grocery, but they are thinking of changing to Uptown Foods. Compare prices for the family's grocery bill and see which store would save them more.

Product	Northwest	Uptown
Orange juice (1 gal.)	2.12	1.95
Flour (10 lbs.)	2.35	2.59
Bread (1 loaf)	.98	1.05
Milk (1 gal.)	1.65	1.69
Bananas (1 lb.)	.45	.38
Cheese (1 lb.)	1.19	1.05
Chicken (cut up)	2.65	2.59
Cereal (12 oz.)	3.68	3.45
Hamburger (1 lb.)	2.12	2.10
Sandwich meat	1.98	2.04
Sugar (5 lbs.)	3.00	2.65
Frozen pizza (medium)	3.65	3.25
Butter (1 lb.)	2.45	2.56
Lettuce (1 head)	.65	.59
Celery (1 lb.)	1.04	1.12
Diapers (1 box)	5.25	5.35
Soda (2-liter bottle)	1.09	.88
TOTAL	_____	_____

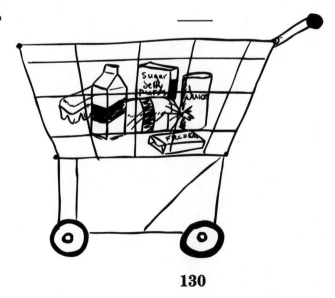

© 1995 by The Center for Applied Research in Education

The Family

NAME _____

The Alvarez Family Budget

Directions:

The Alvarez family budget is listed below. How much do the parents make each month? How much does the family spend? Can you think of three ways to help the family save money?

	Earnings
Mr. Alvarez	2,805.00
Ms. Alvarez	2,805.00
TOTAL	_____

Item	Expenses
Rent	925.00
Water	185.00
Electricity	165.00
Gasoline (for car)	65.00
Car payment	225.00
Credit card payment	200.00
Day care	388.00
Groceries	848.00
College tuition (for Hazel)	539.00
Natural gas (for oven)	75.00
Clothing	365.00
Cable TV	35.00
Savings	280.00
Taxes	1150.00
Car Insurance	115.00
Homeowners Insurance	50.00
Total	_____

List three ways they can reduce their expenses.

1._____

2._____

3._____

The Family

NAME _____

My Relative's Biography

Directions:
Interview a relative who is over 40 years of age and use the information to write a biography.

My Biography of

_____

_____ was born _____
                (name)   (date)

in _____ in the state of _____.
       (town or city)   (state)

When _____ was young (he/she) did something (he/she) was very proud of.
        (name)

_____

_____

Three other things that _____ has done are
                                   (name)

1. _____

2. _____

3. _____

I'm most proud of _____ because (he/she) is my
                            (name)

_____!
 (How are you related?)

© 1995 by The Center for Applied Research in Education

Social Studies

The Family

TIYOSPAYE
(a teacher-led activity)

1. The objective of this activity is help children see that "FAMILY" means different things to different cultures.

2. Introduce the Family Map. Understanding this concept is necessary so that children will understand the TIYOSPAYE.

3. Explain that first we will map the part of our family that lives in OUR HOME. As I was growing up, mine looked like this:

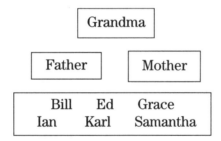

4. Many children will recognize this as similar to their own family configuration. Remember that the oldest generation appears first and the youngest appears last.

5. Give children the Family Map ("Family in a Home") sheet and invite them to draw out their family map.

6. Explain "EXTENDED FAMILY." This includes other relatives who do not live in the home. Again, the oldest generation appears on top, youngest on the bottom.

Here's mine.

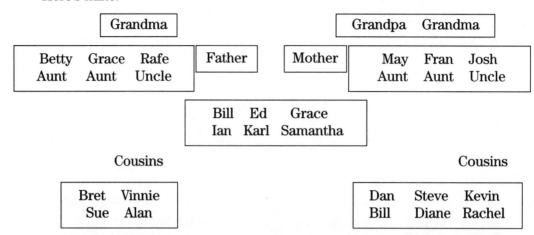

7. Distribute the "Extended Family" worksheet and have the children map out their grandparents, aunts, uncles, parents, siblings, and cousins. If you feel up to it, you might have children include in-laws, aunts, and uncles by marriage. These are *family* maps, not bloodlines, so step-families, blended families, and single-parent families have members equally represented.

8. Explain TIYOSPAYE (pronounced with all long vowels "ti-O-shpī-ay"). Certain Native American peoples (in this case the Dakota people) had an extended family system very different from the one we know. They viewed their mother's sisters as mothers also, and their father's brothers as fathers. Thus, the children of their father's brothers were siblings to them. The children of their mother's sisters were also siblings to them. Cousins were the children of father's sisters and mother's brothers. For example:

Betty Aunt	Grace Aunt	*Rafe Father*	Father	Mother	*May Mother*	*Fran Mother*	Josh Uncle
Cousins	Cousins	*Siblings*			*Siblings*	*Siblings*	Cousins

The reason this extended family model evolved was because life was hard and one often lost a parent to disease, famine, tragedy, or war. This model gave the child comfort and security because if both parents were lost, he or she had another home with parents and siblings. The family remained intact even when members of it were lost. There was no "orphanage" and adoption was necessary only on the rare occasion when a child had no place else to go.

Guide your students to the understanding that this is not strange or weird, but a necessary way to think of "family" for those people. We think of the family differently because our family needs are different. Get children to start thinking about the uncles and aunts who would be their other "parents" and the cousins that would be their "siblings." They will need this for the TIYOSPAYE sheet.

9. Give children the TIYOSPAYE sheet and have them map their own tiyospaye and reflect on the model from their own perspective.

The Family

NAME _____

Family in the Home

Directions:

Listen as your teacher explains a family map. Then make a map of your "family in the home" in the boxes below.

Grandparents

Parents

Children

Social Studies

The Family

NAME _____

Extended Family

Directions:

After your teacher explains how to do it, make a map of your extended family.

My Grandparents

Uncles	Aunts	Father	Mother	Uncles	Aunts

Cousins (Father's Side)	Siblings	Cousins (Mother's Side)

The Family

NAME _____

TIYOSPAYE

Directions:

After your teacher explains a TIYOSPAYE to you, make a map of YOUR tiyospaye. Would you like this? Write your thoughts on the back of this page.

My Fathers would be:

_____

_____

_____

My Mothers would be:

_____

_____

_____

My Brothers and Sisters would be:

_____

_____

_____

My Uncles and Aunts would be:

_____

_____

_____

My Cousins would be:

_____

_____

_____

Social Studies

The Family

A Personal Coat of Arms
(a teacher-led activity)

Purpose:
Generations ago, wealthy families had coats of arms designed especially for them. These crests were created originally for soldiers who needed to be recognized while wearing armor and helmets. Later the crests were embroidered on coats hung over chain mail; thus, the name "coat of arms." These crests were often used by family members on letters, tapestries, and certain items of property. Very wealthy families often had dishes and silverware made with the coat of arms on them. These were handed down from father to firstborn for generations.

Today few families recall their ancient coats of arms. This activity gives children a chance to create a family crest.

Procedure:
Each crest should have three parts: a mantel (or feather plume), a shield, and a banner on which the family name or motto appears. These can be made in any shape or size the child may wish, but some that are common on traditional crests are shown here.

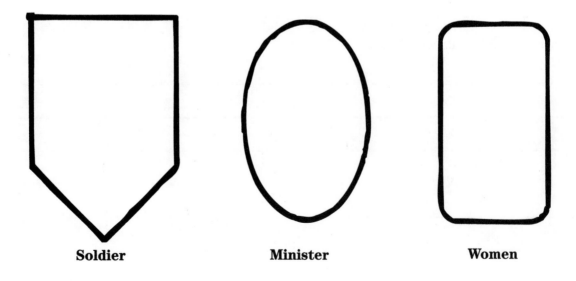

Soldier   **Minister**   **Women**

The mantle is placed above the shield and the banner beneath. On the shield itself the child should design a composition that features symbols representing his or her family story and some characteristics of the family. Here's an example of mine:

Circus

Boys and Girls of All Ages...

Even when I was in elementary school, we all looked forward to the annual spring visit of the traveling circus. So anxious were we that our teachers wisely chose to decorate the room in circus motif, read to us from books about circuses, and arrange a circus art project for Friday when we were so anxious to go see the clowns, elephants and acrobats that we could hardly contain ourselves. Interestingly, I remember few other weeks in my elementary school experience with the same clarity as Circus Week.

Follow these thematic pioneers' example and save the Circus Theme until a circus is coming to town. The children will be most excited and willing to learn then. Take the bibliography provided here to your local library and gather all the circus books you can find. Put up the bulletin board in advance to pique the children's interest. When the time is right to introduce the theme, invite children to vote for their favorite circus act and use the bulletin board as an impetus for a discussion to find out: (1) What they KNOW about the circus, (2) what they WANT to know about the circus, and (3) after the theme week is over, what they LEARNED about the circus. (The KWL approach to content learning.)

# Circus Bibliography

Ambrus, V. *Mishka.* **New York: F. Warne Publishers, 1978 (24 pages).** Misha is an eight-year-old violinist who seeks fame and fortune by joining a circus.

Barton, B. *Harry Is a Scaredy-Cat.* **New York: Macmillan, 1974 (32 pages).** Harry is afraid of everything, but when he is taken into the air by a bouquet of circus balloons he learns something important.

Berenstain, S., and Berenstain, J. *C. Is for Clown: A Circus of C Words.* **New York: Random House, 1972 (35 pages).** A circus act is described using only words starting with "C."

Bond, M. *Paddington at the Circus.* **New York: Random House, 1973 (32 pages).** Paddington joins the circus and becomes a member of the trapeze act.

Brisville, J. *Big Bear.* **Englewood Cliffs: Prentice-Hall, 1977 (32 pages).** A big bear discovers the friendship he craves at a circus.

Brown, M. *Lenny and Lola.* **New York: Dutton, 1978 (32 pages).** Lenny and Lola have a trapeze act, but split up after an argument. Soon they patch it up and add an amazing trick to their already popular act.

Brunhoff, L. *Babar's Little Circus Star.* **New York: Random House, 1988 (32 pages).** Isabelle discovers that being small is an advantage when performing in a circus.

Corcoran, M. *Night Circus.* **New York: Contemporary Books, 1990 (20 pages).** A child bound for bed says goodnight to the ringmaster, the clowns, and the animals of the circus.

DePaola, T. *Jingle the Christmas Clown.* **New York: Putnam, 1992 (unpaged).** A young clown and a troupe of animals stay behind after the circus moves on and give a special Christmas Eve performance to a poor village.

Dubanevich, A. *The Piggest Show on Earth.* **Boston: Orchard Books, 1989 (32 pages).** A pig couple at a pig circus have an exciting time when she loses her balloon during the Circus Parade.

Du Bois, W. *Bear Circus.* **New York: Viking Press, 1971 (48 pages).** Koala bears find circus equipment in the jungle and use it to put on a circus of their own. But it takes them years to learn what the equipment is for.

Ehlert, L. *Circus.* **New York: HarperCollins, 1992 (unpaged).** An unusual circus with leaping lizards, marching snakes, a bear on a tightrope, and other strange performers.

Ernst, L. *Ginger Jumps.* **New York: Bradbury Press, 1990 (33 pages).** Ginger is a circus dog who is frightened of performing a new trick until the little girl he has been dreaming about comes to help.

Faulkner, N. *Small Clown and Tiger.* **New York: Doubleday, 1968 (64 pages).** The tiger is missing, but only the smallest clown is clever enough to find him.

Freeman, D. *Bearymore.* **New York: Viking Press, 1976 (40 pages).** Hibernating Bearymore the Circus bear can't sleep because he is trying to think up a new act.

Gantos, J. *Rotten Ralph.* **Boston: Houghton Mifflin, 1976 (46 pages).** Ralph is a rotten cat who learns the errors of his ways at the circus—or maybe not!

Goennel, H. *The Circus.* **New York: Tambourine Books, 1992 (unpaged).** The amazing sights at a circus as seen through the eyes of a child.

Gunthorp, K. *Millie at the Circus.* **New York: Doubleday, 1970 (27 pages).** Millie is a cow who is tired of her mundane life. She visits the circus in search of excitement.

Hill, E. *Spot Goes to the Circus.* **New York: Putnam, 1986 (22 pages).** Spot loses his ball behind a circus tent and learns a trick when he goes to look for it.

Hoff, S. *Barkley.* **New York: Harper & Row, 1975 (32 pages)** Barkley is too old to perform his circus act and searches for something else to do.

Hoff, S. *Ida, the Bareback Rider.* **New York: Putnam, 1972 (31 pages).** A bareback horse rider learns that everyone has a place at the circus.

Lochak, M. *Suzette and Nicholas and the Sunijudi Circus.* **New York: Philomel Books, 1979 (29 pages).** After attending a traveling circus, the children decide to organize a circus of their own.

Maestro, B., and Maestro, G. *Busy Day: A Book of Action Words.* **New York: Crown Publishing, 1978 (32 pages).** Several verbs are learned through activities associated with the Circus, such as marching, pulling, laughing, washing.

Moncure, J. *Word Bird's Circus Surprise.* **Chicago: Children's Press (Child's World), 1981 (32 pages).** Children learn simple sight words as Word Bird takes them on a trip to the circus.

Packard, E. *The Circus.* **New York: Bantam Skylark, 1981 (55 pages).** A Choose-Your-Own-Adventure set at a circus.

Panek, D. *Detective Whoo!* **New York: Bradbury Press, 1981 (32 pages).** Strange noises draw Detective Whoo to the circus to investigate.

Peet, B. *Pamela Camel.* **Boston: Houghton Mifflin, 1984 (30 pages).** Pamela is tired of the circus, but finds the recognition she craves at the side of a railroad track.

Pellowski, M. *Clara Joins the Circus.* **New York: Parent's Magazine Press, 1981 (42 pages).** Clara the Cow seeks excitement at the circus, but is hopelessly unsuited to every role the circus has to offer her.

Peppe, R. *Circus Numbers: A Counting Book.* **New York: Delacorte Press, 1969 (32 pages).** Circus acts from one to ten. Excellent for teaching ordinal numbers in a circus theme.

Poulet, V. *Blue Bug's Circus.* **Chicago: Children's Press, 1977 (32 pages).** Blue Bug tries nearly every act in the circus before finally deciding to become a clown.

Rey, M. and Shalleck, A. *Curious George Goes to the Circus.* **Boston: Houghton-Mifflin, 1984 (unpaged).** George becomes the star of the circus after getting in the way of the acrobats.

Wahl, J. *The Toy Circus.* **San Diego: Harcourt Brace Jovanovich, 1986 (32 pages).** One of America's best-loved children's authors has written one of the most delightful circus stories. As a boy drifts off to sleep, the toys in his toy box stage a circus on his bedroom floor.

Wiseman, B. *Morris and Boris at the Circus.* **New York: Harper & Row, 1988 (64 pages).** A moose and a bear attend the circus and become part of the show.

CIRCUS BOOKS I'VE READ

NAME _____

1. _____
   Title
   _____
   Author

2. _____
   Title
   _____
   Author

3. _____
   Title
   _____
   Author

4. _____
   Title
   _____
   Author

5. _____
   Title
   _____
   Author

Lenny and Lola
by
Marcia Brown

NAME _____

Directions:

Lenny and Lola had a misunderstanding. Pretend that you are friends with Lenny and Lola. Write a letter to them to try to help them become friends again. Use complete sentences and be sure to check for mistakes after you get your ideas written down.

DEAR _____

_____

_____

_____

_____

_____

_____

_____

_____

_____

_____

_____

_____

_____

_____

_____

_____

_____

Lenny and Lola
by
Marcia Brown

NAME _____

Directions:

After reading the story, fill in the story map below. Use complete sentences for your answers.

Characters	Setting

Why did they argue?	How did it end?

Did you like it?	Why?

The Toy Circus
by
Jan Wahl

NAME _____

Directions:

After reading the story, fill in the story map below. Use complete sentences for your answers.

Characters	Setting

What happened?	How did it end?

Did you like it?	Why?

Clooney the Clown
by Shel Silverstein
(from *A Light in the Attic*)

NAME _____

Directions:

Pretend you are Clooney the Clown. Write a letter to a friend and tell him or her what happens. Tell your friend how you feel about it and what you hope will happen the next time the circus comes to town.

Come to the Circus!
a poem by Karl A. Matz

On Monday I was a circus clown,
my nose was round and red.
I ran around in baggy pants
with an orange wig on my head.

On Tuesday I tamed a lion
in a cage with iron bars.
Everyone clapped when the lion roared
and I was their favorite star.

On Wednesday I was an acrobat
flying through the air.
The people watched from far below
as the wind blew through my hair.

On Thursday I was a juggler,
juggling dressers and chairs.
I juggled a dozen things at once
while the audience sat and stared.

On Friday I played the trumpet
in the famous circus band.
I played for queens and princes
and traveled all over the land.

You might wonder at all the things
that I can be and do.
Just use your imagination
and you can do them too!

NAME _____

Circus Words

Directions:

Think of a circus word for each letter below. The letter can be anywhere in the word. The **O** word is done for you.

L
_____

I
_____

R O A R
_____

N
_____

T
_____

A
_____

M
_____

E
_____

R
_____

Fill in the Words

> ringmaster   trapeze   tickets   costume
> acrobats   clowns   tents
> audience   elephant   parade

The World's Greatest Circus came to town. Miko and Ryan watched as the big, colorful _____ were put up.

"I want to see the people swinging on the _____," said Miko.

"I like the funny _____ best", said Ryan. "They make me laugh when their big pants fall off or when their cars explode."

Miko and Ryan watched and waited until it was time for the circus to begin. When the time came at last, they were the very first ones in line to buy their _____.

They sat together close to the center ring and watched with wide eyes as all the circus performers marched in a grand _____ . Suddenly a huge, grey _____ sat up on his rear legs and made a noise like a loud trumpet. Miko felt the floor shake as the big animal came back down.

Soon the _____ announced the first act and the show began. Miko and Ryan saw lions and tigers, balancing seals, and graceful _____ .

When the last act was announced, Ryan was disappointed. "Already?" he grumbled.

"Well," said Miko looking at her watch, "it has been three hours."

"Three hours?" Ryan was surprised. "Time sure flies when you're having fun."

NAME _____

Follow the Directions

Read and follow the directions carefully.

1. Color the clown.
2. Cut out all the circus pictures along the lines.
3. Paste the clown in the big, dark square.
4. Put the lion on the **LEFT** side of the clown.
5. Put the tent on the **RIGHT** side of the clown.
6. Put the seal **BELOW** the lion.
7. Put the elephant **ABOVE** the tent.
8. Now paste your circus pictures down.

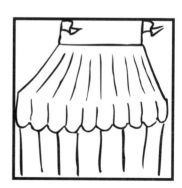

Clown-a-Rounds
(a teacher-led activity)

1. Copy the clown face pattern onto durable cardstock or tagboard and cut it out. Use it to trace a second blank circle on cardstock. Cut the second circle out.

2. Join the two circles in the middle with a brass fastener so that the circle in back can spin.

3. Cut out the mouth (dotted line) so that the surface of the circle in back is visible.

4. Write sight words, spelling words, arithmetic facts, etc., so that they show through the mouth. Turn the back circle until the word you wrote is no longer visible, then write another and so forth until the first word appears again.

5. Provide children with opportunities to study the words or facts in pairs.

6. A useful strategy is to have several numbered Clown-a-Rounds that children work through to mastery, one at a time. When they demonstrate mastery of Clown-a-Round 1, they are rewarded, then they go on to study Clown-a-Round 2, and so forth.

CLOWN-A-ROUND PATTERN

Caring for Your Own Elephant!

The circus was going to leave today but it has to wait for one of the wagons to be fixed. The circus asked you to take care of an elephant for two days. Read all about elephants and answer these questions.

How much food will your elephant need to eat for two days? _____

What kinds of things will you need to feed your elephant? _____
_____
_____

Your elephant is 30 years old. Is this a very old elephant or a very young one? _____
_____

How do elephants keep clean? _____
_____

How much do elephants weigh? _____

What room in your house would be big enough to keep the elephant in? _____
_____

Where might you go to get enough food for your elephant? _____
_____

Armand, the Acrobat
(a teacher-led activity)

Purpose:

Armand is a fun and very inexpensive way to teach the concepts of "center of gravity" and "balance."

Materials:

One prepared Armand for each child (copy onto cardstock or glue to an old file folder and cut out; he needs to be rather rigid)
Box of paper clips

Procedure:

1. Discuss and demonstrate center of gravity and balancing by balancing a meter stick horizontally on your index finger. It will be close to the 50 cm mark.

2. Direct children's thinking with the following questions:

   - What happens if I move my finger to 60 cm? (It overbalances.)

   - What can I do to make it balance at 60 cm? (Add weight to the short arm. Do this and demonstrate the result.)

3. Challenge children to make Armand balance on his nose. (A glue bottle works well as a pedestal.) He can do it, but not by himself. Students will need to realize that Armand is too heavy on top and will overbalance. A paper clip to each hand will balance him, but at a list of about 45 degrees. Two clips to each hand work better. Three clips and he stands straight, tall, and proud.

4. Why did Armand balance when the weight was added? (Guide children to understand Armand was balanced in much the same way as the meter stick was balanced.)

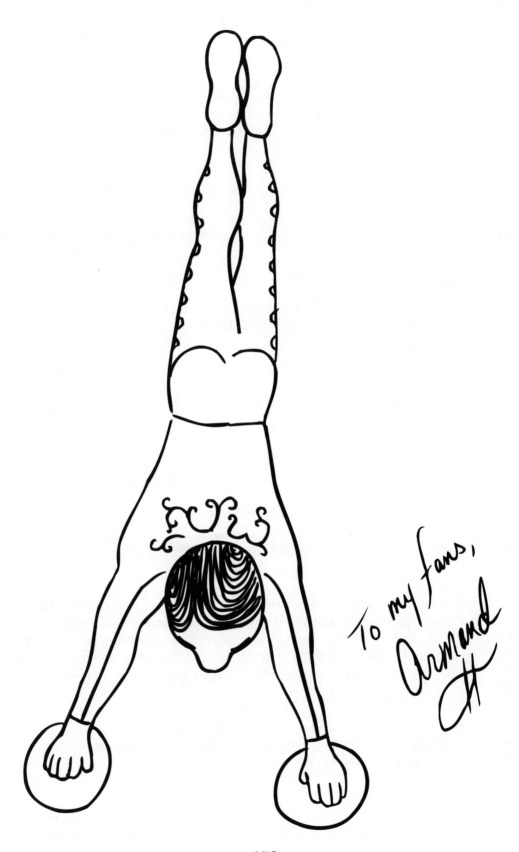

To my fans,
Armand H

 **Circus**

NAME _____

Shapes

Directions:

Color the shape in the picture the same as the shape at the bottom of the page.

159 Math

NAME _____

The Juggling Clown

Directions:

Add the numbers on the clown's juggling balls.

160   Math

NAME _____

The Circus Elephant

Directions:

Solve the addition problems on the circus elephant.

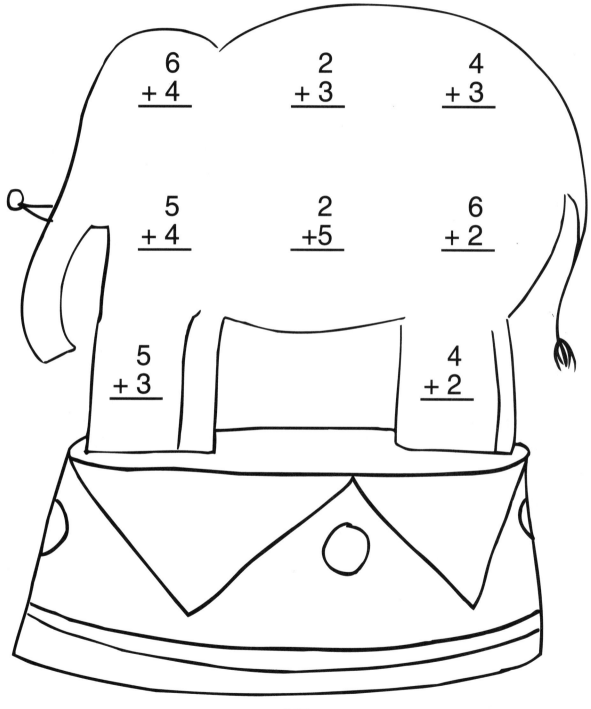

NAME _____

What's the Sum?

Directions:

Add the items. Write your answers in the boxes on the right.

🎪🎪🎪 + 🎪🎪🎪 = ☐

🤡🤡 + 🤡🤡🤡 = ☐

🐘🐘🐘 + 🐘 = ☐

🥜🥜🥜🥜🥜 + 🥜🥜🥜 = ☐

🎈🎈🎈 + 🎈🎈🎈 = ☐

🎟🎟🎟 + 🎟🎟🎟🎟 = ☐

Circus

NAME _____

The Clown's Balloons

Directions:

Use your arithmetic skills to solve the problems below.

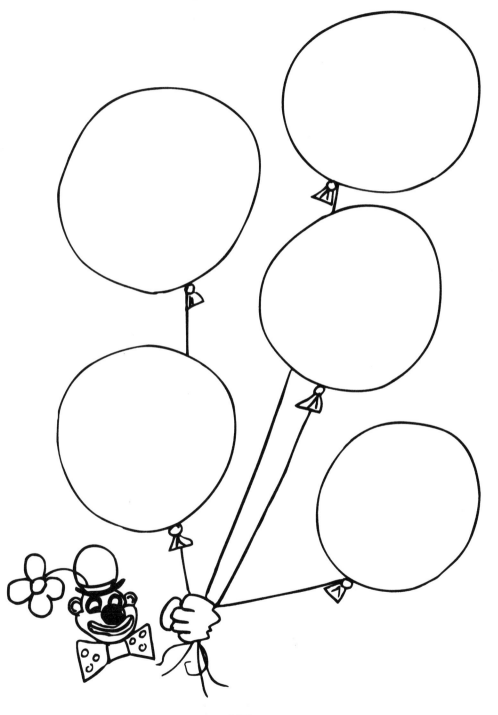

163   Math

NAME_____

Jobs in the Circus

Directions:
Below are six pictures of circus people. What are their jobs? Use the word bank for help. Pick one and use the back of this page to write all you can about the job that person does.

WORD BANK: Lion Tamer   Acrobat   Clown
              Ringmaster   Musician Animal Trainer

NAME _____

Traveling with the Circus

Directions:
Look at a map of your state to help you answer these questions.

1. The circus has its winter home in the largest city in your state. What is the name of that city?

   _____

2. The circus leaves that city every spring and travels east. What is the first town it comes to?

   _____

3. In which direction must the circus travel to get from its winter home to your town?

   _____

4. What are the names of three other towns in your state that the circus might visit?

   _____

   _____

   _____

5. If the circus left your town traveling north, what town would it come to next?

   _____

165

Social Studies

NAME _____

Citizenship

Directions:

How many ways can you think of to be a good citizen at the circus? Make a list of as many ways as you can. One is given to help you get started.

Don't throw things at the animals. Treat the animals kindly.

_____
_____
_____
_____
_____
_____
_____
_____
_____
_____
_____
_____
_____
_____
_____

Find three things in the picture that show good citizenship at the circus.

NAME _____

Let's Make a Poster

Directions:

Make a poster to tell people about the CIRCUS. In the first box write the word CIRCUS in large, colorful letters. In the next box, draw a picture to show people how fun and exciting the circus can be.

FRIDAY AND SATURDAY, JUNE 12 and 13
SHOWS AT 1:00 3:00 5:00 7:00 and 9:00 each day
TICKETS: Adults $5.00 Children $2.50

NAME _____

Laffy the Clown

Directions:

Laffy is a clown. Please help Laffy get ready for the circus. Use your crayons or markers to give Laffy FUNNY HAIR, A RED NOSE, ROSY CHEEKS, EYE MAKEUP, and A BIG CLOWN MOUTH.

© 1995 by The Center for Applied Research in Education

Art

A Theme You Can Really Sink Your Teeth Into!

If this is your first attempt at teaching through themes, a BEAR FAIR is a good theme to start with. "Bear stuff" such as stories, songs, snacks, and trinkets are easy to find and usually very inexpensive. The theme is easy to integrate with art, music, language, science, and social studies. The bear materials in this book will be helpful, but don't be afraid to add to it. The possibilities are as vast as your imagination.

The bulletin board idea offered here is intended to motivate children to read, so it is important that the bulletin board display features book titles that are readily available in the classroom. As children read books, the titles and authors of the books can be written on the "Bear Books I've Read" sheets. These can be copied on various shades of colored paper, cut out, mounted, and displayed on a wall or bulletin board with the title "BEAR-RIFIC READERS!" or some other appropriate title.

While celebrating the bear theme, the children will enjoy observing special days, for example, "Share a Bear Day" in which everyone brings a favorite stuffed bear, "Wear a Bear Day" in which everyone wears an article of clothing or jewelry that has a bear on it, and "Eat a Bear Day" in which bear cookies, gelatin-candy bears, or bear snacks are brought and eaten. An arithmetic activity is included in this book that would be fun and tasty for "Eat a Bear Day." Other observances include "Bring a Bear (picture) Day," "Watch a Bear (movie) Day," "Write a Bear Day," or "Sing a Bear Day."

Bulletin Board Idea

Bears Bibliography

Alborough, J. *Where's My Teddy?* Cambridge, MA: Candlewick Press, 1992 (24 pages). Eddie goes out in search of his teddy who is lost in the woods. As he searches he meets a giant bear with the same problem.

Asch, F. *Bread and Honey.* New York: Parents' Magazine Press, 1981 (34 pages). Ben the Bear paints a picture of his mother with unneeded assistance from Owl, Alligator, Rabbit, and others.

Asch, F. *Moondance.* New York: Scholastic, 1993 (32 pages). A bear dreams of dancing on the moon—and his dream comes true!

Bellows, C. *The Grizzly Sisters.* Toronto: Collier-Macmillan, 1991 (unpaged). The Grizzly sisters won't by their mother's instructions to stay away from other animals. When they go too near a group of campers, they understand why their mother said, "No!"

Brett, J. *Berlioz the Bear.* New York: Putnam's Son, 1991 (unpaged). Berlioz the bear and his fellow musicians are due to play for the town ball when the mule pulling their bandwagon refuses to move. A strange buzzing in Berlioz's double bass turns into a surprise that saves the day.

Bucknall, C. *One Bear in the Hospital.* New York: Dial Books for Young Readers, 1991 (32 pages). Ted Bear is in the hospital with a broken leg.

Carlstrom, N. W. *How Do You Say It Today, Jesse Bear?* New York: Macmillan, 1992 (unpaged). A trip through the year from January to December told in rhyme and pictures.

Christian, M. *Penrod's Picture.* New York: Macmillan, 1991 (48 pages). A "Ready to Read" book about a porcupine and a bear who plan and hold a rummage sale, go camping, and plant a garden.

Day, A. *Frank and Ernest.* New York: Scholastic, 1988 (38 pages). An elephant and a bear take charge of a restaurant and learn all the specialized vocabulary of the restaurant business. Includes a glossary.

Day, A. *Frank and Ernest Play Ball.* New York: Scholastic, 1990 (42 pages). The elephant and bear from Frank and Ernest are back. This time they ake over management of a baseball team and learn the specialized vocabulary with the help of a baseball dictionary.

Goldstein, B. S. *Bear in Mind: A Book of Bear Poems.* New York: Viking Penguin, 1989 (32 pages). A collection of brief and very useful poems about bears.

Hague, K. *Numbears: A Counting Book.* New York: H. Holt. 1986 (32 pages). A group of bears engaged in a variety of activities introduces the numbers one through twelve.

Hennesey, B. G. *Corduroy's Christmas.* **New York: Viking, 1992.** Corduroy trims the tree, bakes cookies, wraps the gifts, and has a delightful Christmas with his friends.

Latimer, J. *James Bear's Pie.* **New York: Charles Scribner's Sons, 1992 (unpaged).** Bear's animal friends try to rescue him when he becomes trapped in his giant, freshly baked pie.

McCully, E. A. *The Evil Spell.* **New York: Harper & Row, 1990 (32 pages).** Edwin Bear is an actor, but when he gets his first major role he gets stage fright on opening night.

McCully, E. A. *Speak Up, Blanche!* **New York: Harper Collins, 1991 (32 pages).** Stagestruck Blanche would like to be a part of a theatrical bear troupe's new play, but her shyness causes problems until she discovers a special talent of her very own.

McPhail, D. *Lost!* **New York: Little Brown and Co., 1990 (unpaged).** A small boy finds a sad bear who is lost in the big city. Together they look for the bear's home.

Nims, B. *Where Is the Bear in the City?* **Morton Grove, IL: A. Whitman, 1992 (22 pages).** Like the "Find Frank" books, the reader looks for a bear in city events like a baseball game, at a subway stop, and among the people on the street.

Radford, D. *Bernie Drives a Truck.* **Cambridge, MA: Candlewick Press, 1992 (unpaged).** Bernie Bear drives his truck and introduces readers to parts of the truck and the work of a truck driver.

Rikys, B. *Red Bear.* **New York: Dial Books for Young Readers, 1992 (unpaged).** Color words are taught as Red Bear dresses, feeds his pet, and goes outside to play. Color names appear on each page.

Ryder, J. *The Bear on the Moon.* **New York: Morrow Junior Books, 1991 (unpaged).** Relates how the great white bears that live at the top of the world came to live on ice and snow.

Scheffrin-Falk, G. *Another Celebrated Dancing Bear.* **New York: Scribner's, 1992 (32 pages).** Boris receives dancing lessons from his friend Max, a dancing bear with the Moscow Circus.

Schoenherr, J. *Bear.* **New York: Philomel Books, 1991 (32 pages).** A little bear learns about life and about himself while searching for his mother.

Schumacher, C. *A Big Chair for Little Bear.* **New York: Random House, (1990). (28 pages).** Little Bear is tired of always having the littlest of everything (chair, bowl, and bed). He wants to try his father's big chair, big bowl and big bed.

Sundgaard, A. *The Bear Who Loved Puccini.* **New York: Philomel Books, (1992). (unpaged).** Barefoot, a young brown bear in the deep forests of Minnesota, falls in love with the music of Puccini and goes to the city to pursue a career as an opera singer.

Waddell, M. *Can't You Sleep, Little Bear?* **Cambridge, MA: Candlewick Press, 1992 (unpaged).** When bedtime comes, Little Bear is afraid of the dark until Big Bear brings him lights and love.

Waddell, M. *Let's Go Home, Little Bear.* **Cambridge, MA: Candlewick Press, 1993 (32 pages).** When Little Bear is frightened by the noises he hears while walking in the snowy woods, his friend Big Bear reassures him.

Young, R. *Golden Bear.* **New York: Viking, 1992 (unpaged).** Golden Bear and his human companion learn to play the violin, talk to a ladybug, make mudpies, wish on stars, and dream together.

REMEMBER, too, the very popular and easy-to-obtain Berenstain Bears books, as well as other available bear books, including *Blueberries for Sal* by Robert McCloskey.

BEAR BOOKS I HAVE READ

1. _____
   Title
   _____
   Author
2. _____
   Title
   _____
   Author
3. _____
   Title
   _____
   Author
4. _____
   Title
   _____
   Author
5. _____
   Title
   _____
   Author

NAME _____

Lost
by
David McPhail

NAME _____

Directions:

In this story, a lost bear is trying to find his way home. Have you ever been lost? Draw a picture and write a story about the time you were lost.

Little Bear
by
Else Holmelund Minarik

NAME _____

Directions:

Who came to share Little Bear's Birthday Soup? Draw a ring around those who came. Make an X across those who did not.

| *Little Bear* by Else Holmelund Minarik | NAME _____ |

Directions:

Look at each picture below. Color all the pictures that show something Little Bear wore. Then write the word for that thing on the line below the picture.

Bread and Honey
by
Frank Asch

NAME _____

Directions:

Fill out the STORY MAP below as the story is read aloud to you. Use complete sentences.

The story started at Ben's home. Where else did the story take place?	Who did Ben meet?

What did everyone tell Ben to do?	How did the story end?

Corduroy
by
Don Freeman

NAME _____

Directions:

Help Corduroy find his missing button.

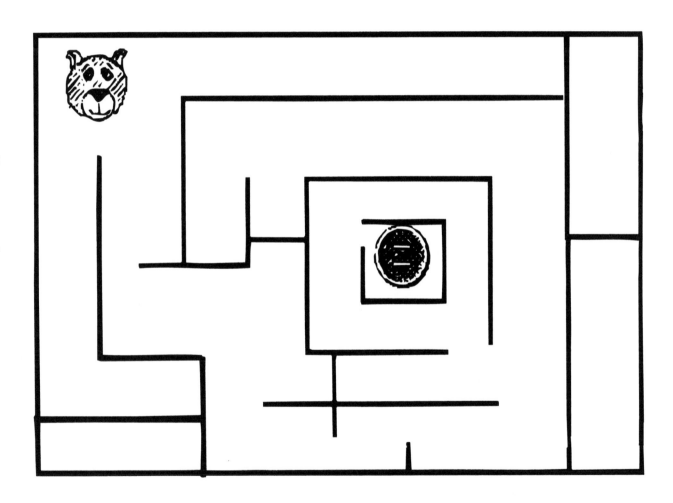

Do You Know This Bear?
A poem by Karl A. Matz

Do you know this bear, my friend?

His hair is white as snow.

He likes to live by the oceanside

Where icy breezes blow.

Do you know this bear, my friend?

He's not a bear at all.

He lives in the mountains of China

Where bamboo grows so tall.

Do you know this bear, my friend?

His hair is dark as night

But on his chest he always wears

A patch of bright sunlight!

Of all the themes herein, music and poetry are most easily available for a BEAR theme. *Bear in Mind,* a book included in the bibliography, has numerous bear poems. "The Adventures of Isabel" by Ogden Nash is a classic favorite for bear themes ("Isabel, Isabel met a bear . . .") as is the action verse "Going on a Bear Hunt." Among the available music is "The Bear Went Over the Mountain," "Teddy Bear Picnic," and "Teddy Bear, Teddy Bear Turn Around." But if you are looking for something different, try Raffi's "Teddy Bear Hug."

NAME _____

Noun-Sense

Directions:
Look at the noun in each box. If it is a plural noun, color the box red. If it is a single noun, color the box blue.

ear	woods	cave
koalas	panda	grizzly bears
honey	berries	cubs
trees	polar bear	claws

NAME _____

Play on Words

Directions:

Write as many words as you can by changing just one letter. The first list has been started to help you.

bear **cave**

tear

NAME _____

Nouns About Bears

Directions:

After you have read *Blueberries for Sal* look through the book to find nouns that name people, places, and things. Try to find five of each kind of noun.

PEOPLE	**PLACES**	**THINGS**

Bear Facts
(a teacher-led activity)

Because bears are often presented as friendly and cuddly creatures, young children sometimes have difficulty understanding that real bears are dangerous wild animals. Here are some facts about bears. Use with the bulletin board to teach children about real bears. The information will also prepare children for the "Bear Facts" worksheet.

- Bears are very dangerous. They will fight to keep strange bears and people off the area they have staked out for themselves. A mother bear will also fight viciously to keep people and animals from coming too near her cubs. Most people who are hurt by bears have simply wandered too close to a bear's territory.
- We shouldn't feed bears because they can get used to snacks and garbage that are not good for them. Bears may "false charge" in order to tell people and animals to leave them alone. They will usually do this only once. Then they will attack. This is only one reason that we should not tease bears. Bears are wild animals and should be treated with caution and respect.
- Bears don't really hibernate. They enter a state of lethargy—a deep sleep.
- Bears have special lips that allow them to pick off berries.
- Bears fish for salmon in fast-moving streams when the fish migrate from June to September. Bears have trouble holding onto slimy fish, so they take them onto land to eat them.
- Bears cooperate with each other during summer fishing and don't fight over territory as they do at other times.
- Bears take only the fish they need. Any part of the fish they don't eat is eaten by the scavengers (some birds, muskrats, bugs).
- Black bears will run away from a fishing spot when grizzlies come to fish. Younger grizzlies will run from older grizzlies.
- Grizzly bears are better fishers than black bears.
- Bears are endangered. There are only about 250,000 black bears left in the USA.
- Bears live in woodlands with berries, wild nuts, fresh water, and fish. These woodlands around the world are being cut down for lumber and to clear land for more farming.

 **Bears**

NAME _____

Bear Facts

Directions:

If you think the sentence says something true about bears, circle the smiling bear. If you think the sentence is *not* true, circle the frowning bear.

1. Bears sleep in winter.

2. Bears wear corduroy overalls.

3. Real bears are very dangerous.

4. Real bears like tacos and candy, just like people do.

5. Bears are wild animals and should not be teased.

6. Bears have special lips that allow them to pick off berries.

7. Real bears should not eat the food we eat because it is not good for them.

8. Bears like to play with people.

9. Bears live in woodlands with plenty of trees and fresh water.

Bears

NAME _____

Food for Bears

Directions:
Cut out the pictures at the bottom of this page and paste them on the boxes below to show a bear's food chain. (Hint: The bear is #6.)

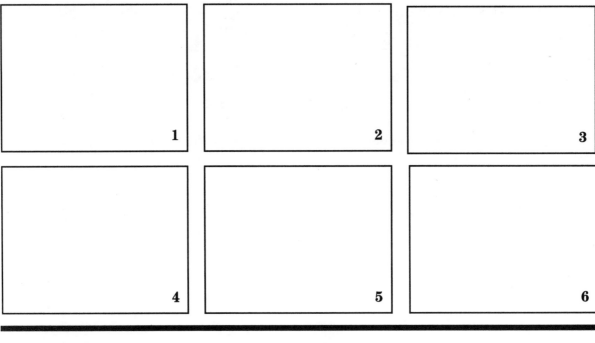

186

Science

© 1995 by The Center for Applied Research in Education

Counting and Sorting Bears
(a teacher-led activity)

Materials:

One packet of gelatin-candy bears for every two students
One copy of "Counting and Sorting Bears" worksheet
One copy of the bear graph sheet for each pair
Paper towels
Crayons

Procedure:

1. Organize children into pairs. It is useful, if you choose to do so, to have one child serve as the sorter/counter and the other as the grapher/colorer. Also, if you intend to let them EAT the candy bears when they are done, it is advisable to have them wash up before handling the bears.

2. Children will open their packets and carefully pour the bears onto a paper towel.

3. Children will sort the bears by color into separate piles, completing the accompanying worksheet. Children should count the number of bears in each color group and record their findings on their graph (sheet).

4. As the pairs begin to finish their tasks, ask them to tell you the total count of the bears in their packet. Record this number on the chalkboard, overhead, or chart paper.

5. List the numbers with the smaller numerals on the left. When numerals are repeated, "stack" them as shown here.

			23	24			
			23	24	25	26	
		22	23	24	25	26	27
21		22	23	24	25	26	27

6. Invite the groups to identify the following:

   - Which number occurred MOST often?
   - Which number occurred LEAST often?
   - What is the DIFFERENCE between the highest and lowest?
   - What is the DIFFERENCE between each pair's number and the HIGHEST?
   - What is the DIFFERENCE between each pair's number and the LOWEST?

7. Finally, of course, invite the children to eat their bears.

Math

Bears

NAME _____

Counting and Sorting Bears: Graph Sheet

Directions:
Color the bears below to show how many of each color you have.

RED

GREEN

ORANGE

YELLOW

WHITE

                1   2   3   4   5

© 1995 by The Center for Applied Research in Education

NAME _____

Counting and Sorting Bears

Directions:

Open your packet and pour the bears onto a paper towel. Sort them into colors and then count the number of bears in each color group.

1. Which color group has the MOST bears?

2. Which color group has the LEAST bears?

3. List the total number of bears in each color group:

   RED _____
   GREEN _____
   ORANGE _____
   YELLOW _____
   WHITE _____

4. What is the TOTAL number of bears in your packet?

Bears

NAME _____

The Bears' Arithmetic

Directions:

Use your arithmetic skills to solve the bear problems below.

NAME _____

Measure Your Bear

Directions:

To complete this page, you will need a ruler and a teddy bear.

1. How LONG is your bear? _____

2. How big AROUND is your bear's tummy?

   _____
   _____

3. How LONG is one of your bear's arms?

   _____

4. How LONG is one of your bear's legs?

   _____

5. Look at your friend's bear. Who's bear is BIGGER?

   _____

> # *Brown Bear, Brown Bear, What Do You See?*
> by Bill Martin, Jr.

Brown Bear sees many different animals, but what do other kinds of bears see? Write a class book about a spectacled bear, a sun bear, a koala, or a panda as a Social Studies or Science activity.

Procedure:

1. Read *Brown Bear, Brown Bear, What Do You See?* even if the children are already familiar with it.

2. Tell the children that they will write a big book about another kind of bear. Let the children decide which bear to write a book about. You might have them debate, pick two, and vote.

3. Remind children where the bear they choose comes from. Ask them if they can name other animals that kind of bear would see in its homeland. For example, a Spectacled Bear would see the animals of South America. A Sun Bear would see the animals of Indochina. Of course most children will have almost no idea what kinds of animals live in Indochina or South America.

4. List as many bears as the children are able to name, then consult the library to find more. You'll need twelve to fifteen so that pairs of children can write and illustrate a page.

5. Put the names of the animals in a list that will serve as the organization of the book. (For example: mountain goat, llama, vicuna.)

6. Pairs of children will write and illustrate a page for the big book. They will need to know not only their own animal but the next animal on the list. For example: "Mountain goat, mountain goat, what do you see? I see a fuzzy llama looking at me."

7. The final book is bound and shared with the whole class, then with another group. If the children are older, a class of younger children can be the audience.

The end result of this activity is not only literacy learning, but also factual knowledge about several animals and the country they come from. Can YOU name twelve animals that live in Indochina?

NAME _____

Pandas and Koalas

Directions:

Pandas and koalas are the most famous bears, but they are not really bears at all! Choose one and find out what country it lives in. Then, look at a map of that country to answer these questions.

1. I chose to learn about the _____. It lives in the country of
_____.

2. What is the name of the nearest ocean?
_____

3. Find a river and write its name.
_____

4. Find the capital of the country and write its name.
_____

5. Find another city or town and write its name._____

6. Find an island and write its name. _____

7. Draw a picture of the animal you chose in the box below.

NAME _____

Where Does This Bear Live?

Directions:
Read about the six bears below. Write the name of each bear on the map below to show where it lives.

POLAR BEAR: I live near the Pacific Ocean, but only where it is cold.

BROWN BEAR: I live in forests south of the polar bear's lands.

BLACK BEAR: I live in the forests too, but only in the western United States.

SUN BEAR: I live in China, one of the largest countries in the world.

SLOTH BEAR: I live in India and on a little island nearby called Sri Lanka.

SPECTACLED BEAR: I live in South America, on the Andes Mountains.

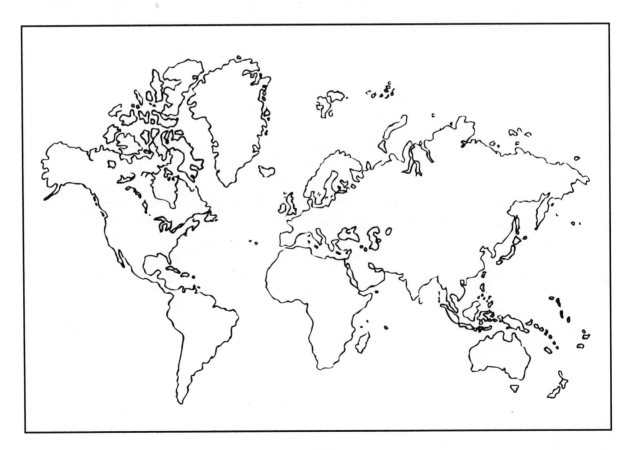

Make a Bear
(a teacher-led activity)

Materials:

Construction paper (1 sheet of brown, two 1" squares of brown, twenty-one 3/4" × 1-1/4" rectangles of white, two 1/2" squares of black, one 1" square of black)
Scissors
Glue
Black markers
Template

Directions for Basic Bear Head:

1. Trace the large peanut shape onto brown construction paper and cut out. This will form the head of the bear.

2. Use the two brown squares to make ears. Cut them to resemble archways or "mouse holes."

3. Use the two white rectangles to make the whites of the eyes. Cut these also to resemble archways or "mouse holes."

4. Use the two small black squares to make the pupils of the eyes. Cut them to resemble pies with a single slice missing.

5. Use the large black square to make a nose. Cut it to look like a triangle.

6. Attach the ears with glue as shown, then attach the whites of the eyes, and carefully attach the black pupils so that the highlight (the "slice") is located in the same place on each eye. Attach the nose so that the triangle points downward.

7. From the point of the nose, draw a short, straight downward line. Draw a smile which touches this line.

Now Make It Your Own:

Children may make the "basic bear" their own by adding those features that will give it character—some hair, a moustache, various hats, suggestions of clothing, eyeglasses, etc. Encourage the children to be creative.

BEAR TEMPLATE

Bears

Bear Necklaces
(a teacher-led activity)

Materials:

Bear cookie cutters
Rolling pins
Fun Dough (recipe below)
Variety of food colors
Colored cord
Newspaper or wax paper

Procedure:

1. Make "Fun Dough" by bringing 1-1/3 cups of water and 1 cup of salt to a boil. Allow to cool, then make dough by adding 4 cups of flour. Add food coloring and knead well for 7 to 12 minutes.

2. Give children balls of colored Fun Dough and instruct them to flatten them and roll out into a thin sheet.

3. Let children use bear cookie cutters to make a Fun Dough "bear cookie."

4. Punch a hole in the top center and place on newspaper or wax paper to dry. Turn them first thing each morning and last thing each afternoon for five days.

5. Run a cord through the hole. Use a short cord for an ornament or a long cord for a necklace.

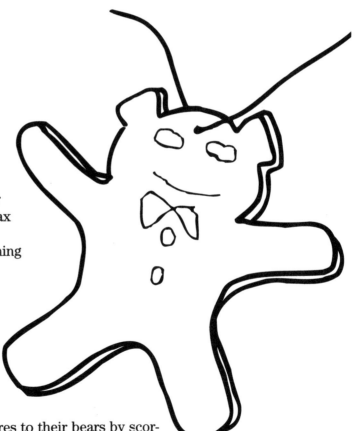

MAKE IT YOUR OWN:

While still wet, children can add features to their bears by scoring them lightly on the surface. Eyes, noses, smiles, and buttons help to make the bears unique, special, and personal.

Farms

A Crop of "Tasty" Activities

The farm theme can be used with rural and urban children alike. Children in small towns—and even in rural areas—may know a great deal about the farms in their region, but they may know little about how farm products get to store shelves or what other kinds of farms are found in other places.

Urban children will profit from an integrated exploration of farms and farming simply because the knowledge will extend their awareness of the wider world and provide some useful science and social studies awareness.

The scavenger hunt is a good way to introduce the theme. Children often have little idea where certain products come from, and this is often due to the fact that they haven't really given it any thought! The scavenger hunt will provide a context for thinking about farms and farm products.

Bulletin Board Idea

Bibliography

Andrews, J. *The Auction.* **New York: Macmillan, 1991 (32 pages).** As the farm is put up on the auction block, Todd and his grandfather make a scarecrow and share stories of bygone days on the farm.

Brandenburg, F. *Cock-a-Doodle-Doo.* **New York: Greenwillow, 1986 (24 pages).** The people and animals on the farm all communicate in their own way: "quack," "neigh," "moo," and so forth. A good book for inspiring a study of animal communication.

Cook, B. *All About Farm Animals.* **New York: Doubleday, 1989 (40 pages).** A good introduction to farm animals and the farm way of life.

Fiday, B. *Time to Go.* **San Diego: Harcourt Brace Jovanovich, 1990 (32 pages).** Leaving the farm is difficult for a boy who was born and grew up there.

Finifer, G. *Ask About Farm Animals.* **Milwaukee: Raintree Publishing, 1987 (unpaged).** In question-and-answer format, this book presents information about a variety of farm animals. Offers a bit more detail than other books of its kind. Good source book for science.

Freedman, R. *Farm Babies.* **New York: Holiday House, 1981 (38 pages).** Many illustrations and sparse text reveal facts about babies of common farm animals.

Gemming, E. *Born in a Barn: Farm Animals and Their Young.* **New York: Coward, McCann & Geoghegan, 1974 (unpaged)** The birth, growth, care and feeding of baby farm animals. A more factual and informational approach than many "baby farm animal" books provide.

Gibson, B. *The Story of Little Quack.* **Boston: Little, Brown & Co., 1991 (32 pages).** Little Quack is Jackie's pet, but one day he disappears! A fun mystery.

Hamilton, V. *Drylongso.* **San Diego: Harcourt Brace Jovanovich, 1992 (52 pages).** A strange tale of a boy who blows into a farm family's home on a dusty drought-laden wind.

Hart, A. *Farm Animals.* **New York: Franklin Watts, 1982 (32 pages).** A very easy fact book. Excellent for providing for a variety of skill levels. Much information about farm animals for less able readers.

Hill, E. *Spot Counts 1 to 10.* **New York: Putnam, 1989 (14 pages).** Spot counts the animals on a farm. Also look for *Spot Visits the Farm* by the same author.

Kent, J. *Little Peep.* **Englewood Cliffs, NJ: Prentice Hall, 1981 (unpaged)** The farm animals all respect the old rooster because he brings up the sun. Little Peep doesn't believe it!

Lewiston, W. *Going to Sleep on the Farm.* **New York: Dial Books, 1992 (unpaged).** A father explains to his son how each animal on the farm falls asleep.

Lindbergh, R. *The Day the Goose Got Loose.* **New York: Dial Books, 1990 (32 pages).** When the old goose gets loose, the farm is in a state of chaos!

Lyon, G. *A Regular Rolling Noah.* **New York: Bradbury Press, 1986 (32 pages).** Intriguing tale of a boy who is put in charge of a boxcar full of farm animals.

Martin, B. and Archambault, J. *Barn Dance.* **New York: Henry Holt & Co., 1986 (unpaged).** A boy awakens late one night to see animals dancing to the scarecrows' fiddle playing. Bill Martin's wonderful verse makes the book extra special.

Mayne, W. *Tibber.* **Englewood Cliffs, NJ: Prentice Hall Books for Young Readers, 1986 (unpaged).** Tibber is a kitten who has a number of misadventures around the farm.

Moore, E. *Grandma's House.* **New York: Lothrop, Lee & Shepard, 1985 (32 pages).** A little girl enjoys her visit to her grandmother's home in the country.

Most, B. *The Cow That Went Oink.* **San Diego: Harcourt Brace Jovanovich, 1990 (33 pages).** The barnyard animals make fun of a cow that oinks and a pig that moos until each teaches its sound to the other.

Nakatani, C. *My Day on the Farm.* **New York: Crowell, 1976 (29 pages).** One child's experiences during a day's visit to a farm.

Paul, J. *Hortense.* **New York: Crowell, 1984 (40 pages).** Hortense Hen's eggs are missing! All the barnyard animals join in the search, but all they find are a bunch of chicks.

Pfloog, J. *Animal Friends and Neighbors.* **New York: Golden Press, 1973 (67 pages, mostly large colored photos).** Introduces many animals, some common to farms and others not so common.

Pinckney, G. *Back Home.* **New York: Dial Books, 1992 (40 pages).** Ernestine, who is only eight, returns to the farm where she was born to visit relatives.

Provensen, A. *Our Animal Friends at Maple Hill Farm.* **New York: Random House, 1974 (57 pages).** The animals on the author's farm include pigs, sheep, cats, goats, chicken, cows, and more.

Provensen, A. *The Year at Maple Hill Farm.* **New York: Random House, 1978 (32 pages).** Seasonal changes on the upstate New York farm that was highlighted in *Our Animal Friends at Maple Hill Farm.*

Rice, E. *At Grammy's House.* **New York: Greenwillow, 1990 (32 pages).** Two children, a brother and sister, spend a fun and interesting day at their grandmother's farm.

Tafuri, N. *Spots, Feathers and Curly Tails.* **New York: Greenwillow, 1988 (32 pages).** Highlights the outstanding features of several farm animals. In question-and-answer format.

Tresselt, A. *Wake Up, Farm!* **New York: Lothrop, Lee & Shepard, 1991 (unpaged).** The morning sounds and activities of animals on a farm.

Turner, D. *Animals and Man.* **Minneapolis: Dillon Press, 1986 (32 pages).** Information about many animals from both farms and fields.

Waddell, M. *Farmer Duck.* **Cambridge, MA: Candlewick Press, 1992 (unpaged).** A duck takes over the chores on the farm because the farmer is too lazy to do so. When Farmer Duck collapses from overwork, the other animals drive the lazy farmer out of town.

BOOKS I'VE READ ABOUT FARMS

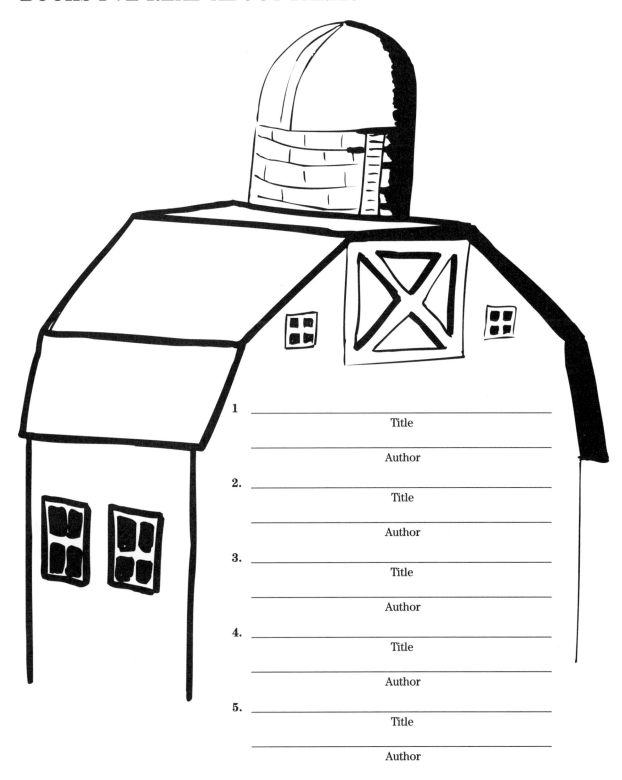

1. _____
   Title
   _____
   Author
2. _____
   Title
   _____
   Author
3. _____
   Title
   _____
   Author
4. _____
   Title
   _____
   Author
5. _____
   Title
   _____
   Author

NAME _____

The Auction
by
Jan Andrews

NAME _____

Directions:

In each box draw a picture of one of the characters from *The Auction*. Write the character's name and a word to describe that character.

Tibber by William Mayne

NAME _____

Directions:

Fill in the farmer's silo by writing the answers to the questions below.

1. Who's the main character?
2. What word best describes the main character?
3. What's the setting of the story?
4. What's the main problem of the story?
5. What is one event you remember from the story
6. Who's another character in the story?
7. Does the story have a "bad person"? If so, who?
8. What was the solution to the problem?

Time to Go
by
Beverly Fiday

NAME _____

Directions:

In each box write the name of one of the characters from the story. On the lines below, write words that describe that character.

Drylongso
by
Virginia Hamilton

NAME _____

Directions:

Look at the words from *Drylongso* in the box below. Decide which words are names for something, which words describe something, and which are words for actions.

Lindy	barefooted	Mamalou	rain	dusty	sweat
running	brown	coughing	drought	planting	sunshine
resting	topsoil	cultivating	moon	working	
July	water	sweetest	shovel	trickling	

Names something	Describes something	Words for actions

207

Reading/Language Arts

 **Farms**

A Letter for Aunt Minnie

Directions:
Find good describing words to make the letter below more interesting. Write them in the blanks.

Dear Aunt Minnie:

It was sure a _____ day yesterday! The sun was shining and the pasture had _____ grass. Dad said we could have a picnic. We filled a _____ basket with _____ food and brought a _____ tablecloth. We found a _____ place by a _____ tree in the north field. That's where that family of _____ birds lives. Every morning we can hear them sing their _____ song. We had some _____ chicken and Dad said, "Why this is _____ pie!" He was right. I know because I made it myself. After we ate we played a _____ game of baseball. I pitched. I am a _____ pitcher. At least that is what Dad said. It was a _____ day. I wish you could have been there.

Your _____ niece,

Annie

© 1995 by The Center for Applied Research in Education

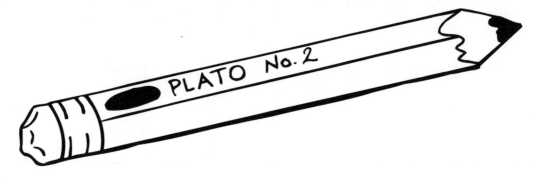

Reading/Language Arts

 **Farms**

NAME _____

Vocabulary

Directions:
Joe has only been a farmer for about a week. He really doesn't know much about it. He makes a lot of mistakes when he talks. Help Joe by underlining his mistakes and writing the correct word in the box.

I went out to the red born.	
I malted the cows.	
After dimmer, I plowed the field.	
I put a saddle on the house.	
Then I had to feed the pegs.	
The ears of can are growing big.	
I like being a former.	

Language Arts

What Shall We Do on the Farm Today?
A poem by Karl A. Matz

What shall we do on the farm today?
Shall we do all the chores or go out to play?

Shall we mend the fences or swim in the lake?
We have an important decision to make.

Shall we milk the cows or dance in the wheat
As the soft earth warms and kisses our feet?

Shall we clean out the barn or roll down the hill?
It's eighty feet long, a wonderful thrill!

Shall we feed the pigs or watch the corn grow
and play hide and seek in the long green rows?

There are so many things for a farm kid to do,
I wish I could be a farm kid too!

© 1995 by The Center for Applied Research in Education

Mrs. Cornbloom's Farm
by Karl A. Matz
(a teacher-led activity)

Directions:

Here is a flannel board story about some important farm animals we often forget. Use the patterns as you tell this story to the children.

Everyone knows about Mrs. Cornbloom's lovely farm. It is the most beautiful farm around. Mrs. Cornbloom grows beautiful flowers, vegetables, and fruits on her farm. She looks after them with great love and care.

One day as she was watering her flowers she saw a bright green frog. "Oh, my!" said Mrs. Cornbloom. "A slimy green frog in my lovely flowers!" She ran into her house and came back with a box. "I will put the frog in this box," she decided. "When I am finished with my work, I will take him far away from my beautiful farm." She put the box on the ground and went back to work.

But as she was hoeing around her vegetables, she saw a lizard. "Oh, my!" said Mrs. Cornbloom. "A slimy green lizard in my lovely vegetables!" She ran into her house and came back with a jar. "I will put the lizard in this jar," she decided. "When I am finished with my work, I will take the frog and the lizard far away from my beautiful farm." She put the jar on the ground next to the box and went back to work.

But as she was raking around her fruit trees, she saw a garden snake. "Oh, my!" said Mrs. Cornbloom. "A slimy green garden snake in my lovely fruit trees!" She ran into her house and came back with a can. "I will put the snake in this can," she decided. "When I am finished with my work, I will take him far away from my beautiful farm." She put the can on the ground next to the jar and the box and went back to work.

But soon she felt a buzzing in her ear. "Bugs?" Mrs. Cornbloom said. "There have never, ever been bugs on my farm!" She turned and saw bugs in her flowers, munching on the leaves. She saw bugs in her vegetables, chewing on the stems. She saw bugs in her fruit trees, crunching on the bark.

"Oh, no!" she cried. "Bugs! Bugs! Bugs! They are eating my flowers, my vegetables, and my fruit. Oh, what shall I do? What shall I do?" She ran around the farmyard swinging her arms and swatting at the bugs but there were too many of them. "They are destroying my beautiful farm!" she cried. Just then she tripped over the box, the jar, and the can.

The frog got loose and hopped into the flowers. The lizard got loose and crawled into her vegetables. The garden snake got loose and slithered into her fruit trees.

"Oh, my!" Mrs. Cornbloom cried. "Frogs, lizards, snakes, and bugs in my flowers, vegetables, and fruit! What shall I do? What shall I do?"

But the frog ate the bugs in the flowers, The lizard ate the bugs in the vegetables, and the garden snake ate the bugs in the fruit trees. Soon there was not one bug to be found on Mrs. Cornbloom's farm.

Now, when Mrs. Cornbloom waters her flowers, she smiles at her friend the frog. When she hoes her vegetables, she winks at her buddy the lizard. When she rakes her fruit trees, she nods at her pal the garden snake. There hasn't been a single bug on Mrs. Cornbloom's farm from that day to this.

Patterns for "Mrs. Cornbloom's Farm"

A Recipe for Beef Stew

Beef Stew

1 pound of beef	2 sliced carrots
1 tablespoon of butter	1 chopped green pepper
3 cups of hot water	1 chopped onion
1 potato, cut into cubes	1 cup of sliced celery
2 tablespoons of flour	salt and pepper

Directions:

1. Look at the recipe above. List all the ingredients that DO come from farms. List the ingredients that you think MIGHT come from farms. List all the ingredients that DON'T come from farms.

DO	MIGHT	DON'T

2. Put each ingredient in its food group.

Dairy	Grain	Meat	Fruit & Vegetable

Farms

An Integrated Activity for Oatmeal Pancakes
(a teacher-led activity)

Materials:

A large mixing bowl, measuring cups, mixing spoons, and an electric grill. For eight 4-inch pancakes (multiply as required):

> 1 egg
> 1/2 c. quick cooking oats
> 1/2 c. whole wheat flour
> 3/4 c. milk
> 2 T. vegetable oil
> 1 T. honey
> 3 tsp. baking powder
> 1/2 tsp. salt

Procedure:

1. Write the list of ingredients on the chalkboard, overhead, or easel paper.

2. SOCIAL STUDIES: Ask children to look at the list and, in their heads, pick the ones that come from farms, the ones they THINK might come from farms, and the ones that they are not sure about. Help children identify the farm products and their source, and those which do not come from farms (baking powder, salt).

3. CRITICAL THINKING: Ask children to guess what these ingredients might make if mixed together and cooked. Write the suggestions on the board and when several have been offered, ask the class to vote on which one they think is most probably correct. Count the votes and graph the results. Then announce that the list is a recipe for pancakes.

4. MATH: Put the class into three groups. Inform the children that this recipe will only serve one group. *Pose this problem*: How can we change the recipe to make enough pancakes for everyone? If children have already been introduced to multiplication, use this activity to extend the concept. Challenge children in pairs to "triple the recipe." Check their work. If children are not yet multiplying, use this activity to introduce the concept. Facilitate discussion around the problem until they arrive at the idea that they will have to make the recipe for each group or "3 times."

5. *Ask*: How many eggs will we need? How much flour? Oats? etc.

6. Make the pancakes. You may wish to have children sign up to bring the ingredients, the plates and forks, syrup, beverage, and cups. It saves your budget (or pocketbook) and provides opportunity for real involvement. Then eat the pancakes and enjoy.

7. Pass out the worksheet "Eating the Growing Things."

NAME _____

Eating the Growing Things

Directions:

Think about the parts of plants. Can you think of some plant roots that people eat? What about plant leaves? Write as many as you can think of in the chart below. One each is done for you.

FLOWER	STEM	LEAF	ROOT	SEED	FRUIT
broccoli	celery	cabbage	carrots	peas	apples

NAME _____

Farmer O'Grady

Hi. My name is Farmer O'Grady. Welcome to your first day as a farmhand. Here's a list of things I want you to do today. Have fun!

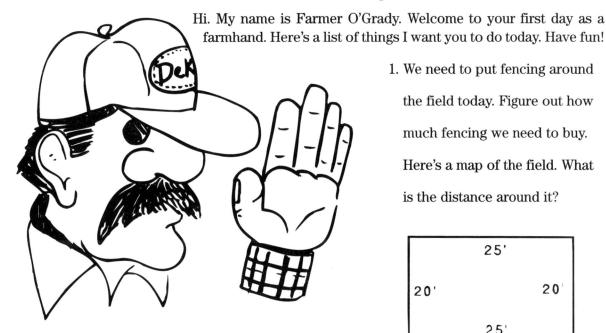

1. We need to put fencing around the field today. Figure out how much fencing we need to buy. Here's a map of the field. What is the distance around it?

2. Fencing is $5.00 a foot. How much will the fencing cost?

   _____

3. We need to put one post every five feet. How many posts will we need?

   _____

4. Posts are $12.50 each. How much will the posts cost? _____

5. We need to put seven nails in each post to hold the fencing in place. How many nails will we need? _____

6. There are eight $100.00 bills on the table in the kitchen. Take them to the lumber yard and buy the fencing and the posts. How much will that cost all together?

   _____

7. How much change will you bring back? _____

The Clever Farmer
(a teacher-led activity)

Directions:

Read this story to the class before giving them the sheet "The Clever Farmer."

Not long ago in a land not far from here, there lived a king. This king loved horses, but he was very greedy and stingy. He was known far and wide as the meanest penny-pincher in the kingdom.

One day he called to his messenger. "I need someone to care for my horses," he said. "Find someone who will do the work VERY cheaply."

The messenger went looking for someone to care for the horses. He returned many days later with a farmer. "This man has worked among horses all his life, Sire. He is an expert on how to care for them."

"Never mind that," the King said. "Is he CHEAP?"

"Sire," the farmer spoke up, "I will agree to work for you for only one penny the first day and two pennies the second day, if you will continue to double my wages everyday for a month. Pay me the last day of the month."

"A whole day's work for only a penny?" the King thought. "And then another day for only two pennies." He laughed to himself. "Why the third day will only cost me four pennies!" How could he refuse?

"I agree!" the King said happily.

"Remember, Sire," the farmer reminded him. "You agree each day to pay double the amount from the day before."

"Yes, yes. I understand," the greedy King smiled.

At the end of the month the farmer returned to the King for his pay. When he told the King how much he owed, the King turned red and his eyes popped. "That can't be!" he thundered.

"Oh, yes," said the farmer. "That is the amount you promised to pay."

How much did the King owe the farmer? Use the calendar on the worksheet to help you figure out the farmer's pay. Remember, each day you double the amount from the day before. The first three days are done for you.

NAME _____

The Clever Farmer

Directions:

Listen to the story "The Clever Farmer." Use this calendar to find out how much the King owes the farmer. The first three days are done for you.

1	2	4				

From a Farm to Your Home

Directions:
You know that corn grows on a farm, but how does it get to your table? Read this seed story and then answer the questions on the next page.

I was born and raised on an ear of corn that grew on Mrs. Cornbloom's farm. She picked me and many of my friends and took us to a buying station. She met Mrs. Nordling, who works as a buyer for a canning company. Mrs. Nordling bought us from Mrs. Cornbloom, then she called Mr. Jacobs, a truck driver, to come and pick us up. Mr. Jacobs put us in big burlap bags and loaded us onto his truck. We rode in the truck to the canning factory. When we got to the canning factory, we saw many trucks just like Mr. Jacobs'. Four men unloaded the trucks and dumped us out of the bags into long deep wagons.

Next, the wagon was taken to a big machine and we were dumped in. First the machine took off our husks. Then we bounced down a belt where Ms. Hermida looked us over to make sure we were good enough to be canned. Some corn that wasn't good enough was sent to another place and made into other products like dogfood and corn oil. The rest of us went down a belt to a machine that took us off the cobs. It felt funny but it didn't hurt at all. We were mixed with water, then cooked. Next we were sealed into many different sizes of cans. I was put into a family size, then 24 cans just like mine were put into a big cardboard box. This was all done by machines. A few days later, Mr. Rafael put us onto a big long truck with a bright, silver box. He drove us to a grocery store in your town. After we got to the grocery store, four people unloaded us from the truck and put us in a room in the back of the store. We sat in our boxes in the back room until night time. Then a man named Mike took us out of the back room and into the store. He opened the box and put me on a shelf. I sat there until you bought me and took me to your house.

NAME _____

From a Farm to Your Home

Directions:

After reading "From a Farm to Your Home," think about which job you would like to have. Which job would you NOT like to have? Tell why.

1. I would like to be _____.

I would like this job best because _____

_____

_____

_____

2. I would not like to be _____.

I would not like this job because _____

_____

_____

_____

Farms

NAME _____

Scavenger Hunt

Directions:

Take a trip to the library. Hunt through books and encyclopedias—and your own brain—to find the farm facts listed below.

1. Corn, wheat, and beans are grown on farms. Find three other plants that are raised on farms.

   _____

   _____

   _____

2. Milk is not a plant, but it also comes from farms. Find and list three other things that are not plants, but still come from farms.

   _____

   _____

   _____

3. Choose one of the plants on your list in number 1 and name three things that are made from it.

   _____

   _____

   _____

4. Choose one of the farm products listed in number 2 and name three things that are made from it.

   _____

   _____

   _____

 **Farms**

NAME _____

What Is It?

Directions:

Draw something to finish the picture.

Art

Habitat
We All Need Each Other

Through a study of habitat we learn about the world around us and our place in it, as well as the interdependence of animals and plants. It's a rich theme with a lot to teach. Included in this collection of activities are science and social studies activities, any of which will serve well to introduce the theme. The introductory activity below has an added dimension. It will extend and activate children's knowledge of habitat and interdependence and provide a rich context for discussing the important aspect of the theme.

Materials:

You will need quart jars in sufficient number to provide one to each group of four students, potting soil, elodea plants (available at tropical fish stores), and bird feed (probably available at the same store).

Procedure:

1. Place two inches of soil in a jar. Add about three inches of water and place the uncovered jar near a window. (Tap water works, but if you can get pond water, so much the better. It will provide some life forms to increase the variables in your habitat.) Let the jar stand for 12–24 hours.

2. Place an elodea plant in the jar.

3. Add three or four seeds of the bird feed every day or two. Do not add water to the jar. While there is standing water in the jar, the seeds will most certainly decompose. Continue adding seeds even when the water has completely evaporated.

4. As the water evaporates, the elodea will become exposed and will die. The seeds will begin to grow when the habitat is appropriate for them. Add water as needed to maintain the environment.

5. As the habitat begins to come to life, discuss what happened. What was needed to get the habitat growing? What conditions prevented the habitat from forming? What did the plants need to grow?

ANIMALS FOR BULLETIN BOARD

Habitat  Bibliography

Arnosky, J. *I Was Born in a Tree and Raised by Bees.* **New York: Bradbury, 1988 (46 pages).** A forest inhabitant named Crinkleroot describes the world around him. Mostly black and white, but a few dazzling color illustrations. Includes activities like growing popcorn, making a birdfeeder and making a leaf book.

Baylor, B. *Desert Voices.* **New York: Scribner, 1981 (32 pages).** A very interesting approach. Desert animals tell about their lives in their own words.

Becker, J. *Animals of the Woods and Forests.* **St. Paul, MN: EMC Corp., 1977 (56 pages).** Color illustrations and intelligent, readable text introduces ten animals that live in the forests and woodlands of the Northern Midwest.

Coatsworth, E. *Desert Dan.* **New York: Viking, 1960 (61 pages).** Older kids can read it, and the teacher can read to the little ones. A fine tale of Dan who roams the desert with his animal friends at his side.

Cortesi, W. *Explore a Spooky Swamp.* **Washington D.C.: National Geographic, 1978 (32 pages).** Content given as a story as two children explore the plants and animals that live in the swamp.

Fatio, L. *The Happy Lion in Africa.* **New York: McGraw-Hill, 1955 (33 pages).** The Happy Lion was a well-loved character in children's books of the 1940's and 1950's. In this one, he is kidnapped and winds up in the African jungle, a place with which he has no experience. Reveals the habitat in a simple way through innocent eyes.

George, J. G. *The Moon of the Wild Pigs.* **New York: Thomas Crowell, 1968 (39 pages).** A gem from the author of *My Side of the Mountain*. Interesting story that explores the habitat of a drought stricken desert through the eyes of a little wild pig trying to survive in it.

Goetz, D. *The Arctic Tundra.* **New York: William Morrow, 1958 (62 pages).** Hard to find, but worth the search. This is one of the few books that presents the rich and varied life found in the sub-temperate north.

Greenaway, T. *Desert Life.* **New York: Dorling Kindersley, 1992 (29 pages).** Color illustrations and simple text describe the variety of life, such as tortoises, insects and crustaceans. that can be found in a desert.

Greenaway, T. *Swamp Life.* **New York: Dorling Kindersley, 1992 (29 pages).** Beautiful color photographs reveal the fascinating and sometimes frightening world of the swamp habitat.

Guiberson, B. *Spoonbill Swamp.* **New York: Henry Holt, 1992 (30 pages).** Spoonbills are ducks that live in the swamps next to alligators and snakes. Learn about the swamp habitat with this wonderful, colorful book.

Hines, A. *Come to the Meadow.* New York: Clarion, 1984 (**unpaged**). Everyone is too busy to accompany Mattie on an exploration of the spring meadow until Granny suggests a picnic.

Hirschi, R. *Who Lives in Alligator Swamp?* New York: Dodd, Mead, 1987 (**31 pages**). Color photographs reveal the habits and habitat of swamp life at dawn in the swamp.

Jasperson, W. *How the Forest Grew.* New York: Greenwillow, 1980 (**55 pages**). A terrific and intriguing discussion of forest habitats told in a story of a forest in New England as it grew over a period of 200 years.

Jernigan, G. *One Green Mesquite Tree.* Tucson, AZ: Harbinger House, 1988 (**21 pages**). Primary. Introduces the numbers 1-20 through use of desert animals and plants and rhyming text.

Johnson, S. *Animals of the Temperate Forests.* Minneapolis: Lerner, 1976 (**28 pages**). The lives and lifestyles of ten animals that live in the northern forests including otters, raccoons, beavers, moose, porcupines, and flying squirrels.

Jordan, M. *Journey of the Red-Eyed Tree Frog.* New York: Green Tiger, 1992 (**unpaged**). Fiction with a healthy dose of fact. A tree frog, trying to save his rainforest home, takes a long journey to the deepest part of the Amazon jungle. We learn about the animals he meets along the way.

Kimmel, E. *Anansi Goes Fishing.* New York: Holiday House, 1992 (32 pages). The jungle habitat is revealed through a story of a tricky spider who is the victim of his own trickery in the end.

Kirkpatrick, R. *Look at Pond Life.* Milwaukee: Raintree, 1978 (32 pages). Easy text and beautiful illustrations explore the life in a common pond.

Naomi, J. *Roadrunner.* New York: Dutton, 1980 (32 pages). A day in the life of one of the desert's most energetic inhabitants.

Paulsen, G. *The Small Ones.* Milwaukee: Raintree (also distributed by Children's Press, Chicago), 1976 (48 pages). A nature journal by one of childhood's favorite authors. Black and white and some color photos and illustrations along with episodic text. Interesting.

Pearce, Q. L. *Nature's Footprints in the Desert.* Englewood Cliffs, NJ: Silver Press, 1990 (24 pages). One of the "Nature's Footprints" series. Not just a description of the animals in the desert, but also interesting discussions of behavior and habits.

Pearce, Q. L. *Nature's Footprints in the Forest.* Englewood Cliffs, NJ: Silver Press. 1990 (unpaged). One of the "Nature's Footprints" series. In this entry, the reader is invited to follow animal tracks into the forest to learn about the animals and plants that live there.

Penney, G. J. *Spikey the Mini Monster.* Waco, TX: Word Books, 1974 (unpaged). Prepare to be charmed by two boys who learn about desert life while pursuing a horned toad named Spikey.

Pollock, S. *The Atlas of Endangered Animals.* **New York: Facts on File, 1993 (58 pages).** An important resource for teachers. Provides a geographical perspective on the issue of endangered animals and reveals the Earth's diverse habitats at the same time.

Pratt, K. *A Walk in the Rainforest.* **Nevada City, CA: Dawn Publications, 1992 (31 pages).** A book with a heavy dose of WOW! The best way to explore the rainforest is to walk through it—and this book will take you there.

Reid, G. *Pond Life: A Guide to Common Plants and Animals of North American Ponds and Lakes.* **New York: Golden Press, 1967 (160 pages).** Descriptions and illustrations of common pond and lake life. A good teacher resource.

Rinard, J. *Wonders of the Desert World.* **Washington, D.C.: National Geographic, 1976 (32 pages).** Beautiful color photography and well-written but simple text reveal the breathtaking and sometimes startling beauty of the southwestern U.S. desert. Many animals and plants are depicted and discussed. A must-read.

Tresselt, A. *The Gift of the Tree.* **New York: Lothrop, Lee and Shepard, 1972, 1992 (unpaged).** A richly illustrated, poignant story of the life and death of a tree that serves as the habitat for a rich diversity of life forms. Don't teach habitats without it!

Weir, B. *Panther Dream: A Story of the African Rainforest.* **New York: Hyperion, 1991 (40 pages).** A must-read. A village boy hunting for food encounters a panther who teaches him the ways of the rainforest.

Whitlock, R. *Penguins.* **Milwaukee: Raintree, 1977 (56 pages).** Nice photography and somewhat sophisticated, but still readable text reveals the arctic habitat through the eyes of one of its dominant lifeforms.

Williams, T. *The Secret Language of Snow.* **San Francisco: Sierra Club, 1984 (129 pages).** The Inuit language has many words for snow. This wonderful book explores the arctic habitat through the vocabulary of Inuit people for the many varieties of snow and snowy weather. Interesting approach, a valuable teacher resource.

Willow, D. *At Home in the Rainforest.* **Watertown, MA: Charlesbridge, 1991 (30 pages).** The rainforest we know best is the South American rainforest. This little book will surprise you with how much there is to learn.

NAME _____

BOOKS I'VE READ ABOUT HABITATS

1. _____
   Title
   _____
   Author

2. _____
   Title
   _____
   Author

3. _____
   Title
   _____
   Author

4. _____
   Title
   _____
   Author

5. _____
   Title
   _____
   Author

I Was Born in a Tree and Raised by Bees
by
Jim Arnosky

NAME _____

Directions:

There's a lot of information about animals in this book. Use the web below to organize the information in the box at the bottom of the page.

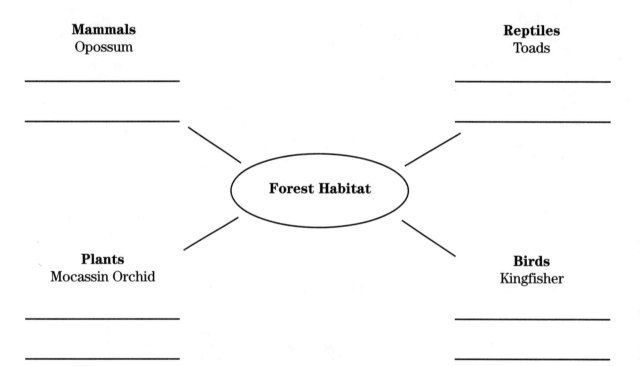

Mammals
Opossum

Reptiles
Toads

Forest Habitat

Plants
Mocassin Orchid

Birds
Kingfisher

Grows in moist bogs   Is the queen bee

Dives for minnows   Eats ants, dragonflies, and bees

Can't move their eyes   Will eat robin's eggs

Come to the Meadow by Anna Grossnickle Hines

NAME _____

Directions:

A meadow is one kind of habitat. List another habitat, such as a forest or desert, and tell what Matty will find there instead.

Matty's Meadow	**Your Habitat:** _____
Monkey flowers and buttercups	_____
A hop toad and pokey old turtle	_____
A nest with three speckled eggs	_____
Crickets singing *cheer-up*	_____
A spider on a thimbleberry bush	_____

The Gift of the Tree
by
Alvin Tresselt

NAME _____

Directions:
The author uses many interesting words in the story of the tree. Read the sentences below and try to think of a more interesting or more descriptive word than the underlined word.

1. Squirrels made their homes in <u>messy</u> bundles of sticks.

   _____

2. Tucked under its <u>old</u> roots, small creatures found safety.

   _____

3. The forest soil increased as <u>old</u> leaves mouldered under the snow.

   _____

4. Termites ate out passageways in <u>good</u> patterns.

   _____

5. Woodpeckers <u>marked</u> the limbs with holes.

   _____

6. The great branches broke and <u>fell</u> to the forest floor.

   _____

Habitat

The Greb-Greb Fish
Traditional: Adapted by Karl A. Matz

Near the island of Al-Di-Loo
In the ocean wide
Lived a little bitty greb-greb fish
With green dots on his side.

He sang as he swam in the ocean,
"Brammle dem rim pom dare
I wish I could live with the birdies
And fly through the fresh, warm air."

On the island of Al-Di-Loo
In the forest wide
Lived a little bitty reff-reff bird
With yellow feathers on his side.

He sang as he sat in an oak tree,
"Brammle dem rim pom pree
I wish I could live with the fishies
And swim in the fresh, cool sea."

But fishies must live in the ocean,
Fins don't work in the trees.
And birdies must live in the open air,
Feathers get wet in the seas.

Habitat

Five Ways to Respond to "The Greb-Greb Fish"
(a teacher-led activity)

1. *Tell the children:* "Draw a picture of the Greb-Greb Fish and the Reff-Reff Bird. How can you show that each wants to live where the other one lives?"

2. *Say:* "Think of two other animals that need different habitats. Rewrite your own version of "The Greb-Greb Fish" using your animals instead of the fish and the bird."

3. *Say:* "You're walking through the forest on the island of Al-Di-Loo and you hear a voice. It's the reff-reff bird and he wants to tell you his life story. He explains why he hates the air and wants to live in the sea. Write the story he tells in his own words."

4. *Primary:* Write the poem on oaktag and post it for a week. Then, cut the poem into sentence strips and scramble. Make it a learning center where children must arrange the strips correctly, then rescramble for the next person.

5. *Upper:* "Can you use your problem-solving skills to invent a way for the fish and bird to exchange habitats? Draw a picture of your solution and write a description and explanation."

Habitat

Drought Comes to the Habitat
(a teacher-led activity)

Materials:

Per Group:
Two healthy bean plants
"Drought Diary"

Background Information:

Help children recall what happens during a drought. Remind them that drought does not mean it NEVER rains, only that it rains too little to meet all the needs of the living things in the habitat.

Hypothesis: What happens to plants when they receive too little moisture?

Procedure:

1. Make sure the plants are properly watered. Place them in a sunny window and observe each day. Record your observations.

    DO NOT WATER EXCEPT WHEN INSTRUCTED TO DO SO.

2. After three days, provide a normal amount of water to the "Normal" plant, but only a film canister full of water to the "Drought" plant.

3. Observe the plants and record your observations each day.

4. Repeat steps 2 and 3 every three days for a total of 20 days.

5. Complete the observations. What happened? Why?

NAMES _____

_____

_____

Drought Diary

Directions:

Record your observations in the boxes below.

Normal Plant	Drought Plant
3 days	
6 days	
9 days	
12 days	
15 days	
18 days	

Habitat

NAME _____

Living and Nonliving Things

Directions:
Look at the picture below. Find the living things in the picture and color them. Leave the nonliving things white.

Habitat

NAME _____

Beaks and Bills

Directions:

Look up various kinds of birds in resource books or the encyclopedia. Look for interesting or unusual beaks. Choose ten that interest you most. Classify your ten birds on the chart below according to the kind of beak they have. Write each bird's name in the box under the beak name.

	Sipper	**Crusher**	**Scooper**	**Pincher**
1				
2				
3				
4				
5				
6				
7				
8				
9				
10				

© 1995 by The Center for Applied Research in Education

Habitat

A Habitat Game
(a teacher-led activity)

Purpose:

This game will demonstrate to children the interdependence of animal life and their environment. At the same time, children will have an opportunity to discuss the issues and compare the results through mathematics.

Procedure:

1. Discuss the basic resources needed by animals in their habitat. What do animals need to have available in their habitat to survive? (food, a source for water, shelter or "cover")

2. Organize the class into four groups. Mark off two parallel lines that are several yards apart.

3. Choose one group to be the animals. The other groups will serve as the resources of the habitat: the food, the water source, and shelter or ground cover.

4. The animals communicate their needs through signs. When looking for food, they place their hands over their mouths. When they are looking for water, they cup their hands as if drinking from a pond. To communicate a need for shelter, they hold their hands (fingers interlaced) over their head. The "animal-players" can choose to look for any of these resources during each round, but they cannot change what they are looking for until the next round.

5. The "habitat-players" choose which of the essential elements they will be. They will depict that resource with the same sign language as the animals.

6. Before the game begins, you should record the number of animals. The game starts with the habitat-players lined up with their backs to the animal-players. Ask all students to choose a signal. At the count of three, the students turn and face each other displaying the signal of the resource they have chosen.

7. The animal-players run to the element of habitat that matches the sign language they are displaying (animal-players in search of food move toward the habitat-players displaying the sign for food, and so forth); animal-players collect that resource, and bring it back from the habitat line to the animal line. In this way, animal-players demonstrate that they have successfully met a need. Any animal-player that fails to find the resource it is seeking must die. Two habitat-players rejoin the habitat group. This represents regeneration of habitat through rainfall and plant growth. The rest of the habitat-players then become animals. This represents reproduction.

8. Play ten or fifteen rounds of the game. You record the number of animals at the beginning and ending of each round.

9. After the game, engage children in a discussion. Guide the students to understand that in the beginning, the resources are plentiful and the herd can grow. As the herd becomes bigger, the resources become more scarce. Some animals must die to maintain the balance in the habitat. This is known as the "balance of nature."

10. **Extension**: Replay with half the habitat players and demonstrate to children what happens when the resources are suddenly diminished. If possible invite another class to help demonstrate to the children what happens to the animals when the resources are nearly unlimited.

11. **Language Arts (Cause and Effect)**: What will happen if drought reduces the water and plant life in the area? What will happen if fires destroy the grasslands? What will happen if uncontrolled hunting is permitted? (The "Ecology" Theme has a story you may find useful here. A town that loves its mule deer destroys all the wolves in the area to protect the deer. They are soon overrun with animals foraging for food.)

12. **Math**: Make a graphic representation of the relationship between habitat and population. With the help of the class, make a graph of the number of animals alive at the end of each round. Compare with a graph of the "number" of habitat-players to demonstrate how reduction of habitat resources must naturally reduce the number of the animals.

13. Replay. You may have a drought, for example. In this case, the habitat-players will not feature any water. Don't tell the animals (animals never really know when a drought is coming or why the water is scarce). The animal-players will not know why there is no water available until after this phase of the game is over. A new graph can then be made to demonstrate the effect of drought upon the balance of nature.

Habitat

NAME _____

The Swineburn Swamp Party

Directions:

The animals in the Swineburn Swamp had a party. Everyone came and a good time was had by all. Solve the story problems, which are based on the five creatures in the party photo below.

1. Larry the Lizard is 29 inches long. His sister is half that length. How long is she? _____

2. Larry is cold-blooded, so he has to sleep until the air temperature is at least 70 degrees. It's 42 right now. How many degrees must it rise before Larry will wake up? _____

3. Freddy the Frog ate 12 flies per hour at the party. He was there for 5 hours. How many flies did he eat?
_____

4. Freddy usually eats only 4 flies per hour. How many flies does he eat in 16 hours?
_____

5. Greta the Gadfly can drink 3 ounces of liquid in one minute. How long would it take Greta to drink a 12-ounce can of soda? _____

6. Rodney Raccoon can walk 2 miles per hour. He can run 3 times that fast. How fast can he run?
_____

7. Rodney lives 14 miles from the pond where the party was held. How long will it take him to walk home?
_____

8. Cecilly the Snake eats a mouse a week. How many mice does she eat in six months? _____

9. Cecilly is six times longer than Larry the Lizard. How long is she?
_____

10. Cecilly's favorite breakfast is a big, fat raccoon. There's no story problem to solve here, but maybe someone should tell Rodney!

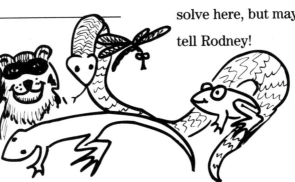

243

Math

Habitat

NAME _____

Can You Help?

YIKES! I lost all my notes! Use reference books to help me locate the sizes and weights of these unusual animals.

Animal	Size	Weight	Habitat
Bison	12 feet long	2400 lbs	Prairie
Ptarmigan	_____	_____	Tundra
Vicuna	_____	_____	_____
Mongoose	24 inches long	_____	Jungle
Parrot	_____	2 lbs	_____
Eagle	_____	_____	_____
Coral Snake	_____	_____	Desert

Challenge:

Make a bar graph comparing the weights of the animals. Use drawings and colors to make it interesting.

© 1995 by The Center for Applied Research in Education

Habitat

NAME _____

What's the Answer?

Directions:

Use your multiplication skills to solve the nine problems below.

```
   12        15        18
  X 11      X 14      X 21


   22        25                 88
  X 16      X 28               X 35


                                56
   38                          X 43
  X 30       44
             X 34
```

245   Math

NAME _____

Habitat

Endangered Animals

Directions:

There are many habitats in the United States where animals are endangered. Look at the list of animals on the left and draw the symbol for that animal on the map.

Ivory-Billed Woodpeckers:
Large forests of Florida, Georgia, and South Carolina

American Lobster:
In the Atlantic Ocean from Connecticut to Virginia

Red Wolf:
South Central U.S. and Texas

California Condor:
California and Nevada

© 1995 by The Center for Applied Research in Education

Habitat

NAME _____

Habitat Temperatures

Directions:

How is the temperature in your habitat different from the temperature in someone else's habitat? Use the graphs below and your local newspaper to find the answer.

Graph 1: My Habitat _____

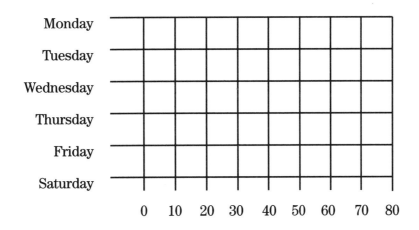

Graph 2: A Habitat Far Away _____

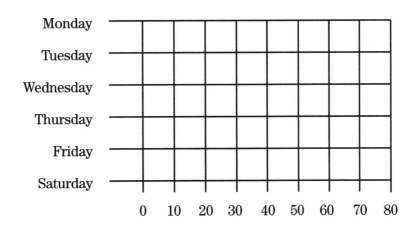

Habitat

NAME _____

Where in the World?

Directions:
Where in the world would you expect to find habitats like these? Name an animal that lives there. One is done for you.

Habitat	Place	Animal
Everglades	Florida	Alligators
Forests	_____	_____
Deserts	_____	_____
Rainforests	_____	_____
Prairies	_____	_____
Mountains	_____	_____
Seacoasts	_____	_____
Lakes	_____	_____

Habitat

Interpreting Reality
(a teacher-led activity)

Purpose:

Some artists create drawings and paintings that are so lifelike it takes your breath away, and others believe that cameras are for the art of realism. An artist, they say, should interpret reality, not replicate it. This is a concept that is difficult to teach to children. The following project will go a long way toward helping children understand how reality can be creatively interpreted.

Materials:

9" X 12" white drawing paper

Glue

A variety of colored construction paper scraps

Lots of wildlife or nature magazines or pictures of animals and scenery

Scissors

Pens

Procedure:

1. Make a model for the children based on the guide below.

2. Each child will need a sheet of white paper, glue, and one or more pictures of animals from magazines. Inform the children that they are going to create a scene from nature using colored paper shapes (as with silhouettes). There are only two rules: (a) students may not use the real color of any object (that is, clouds will not be white, the sky will not be blue, the deer will not be brown), and (b) there can be no sign of human life or civilization.

3. The young artists should find pictures in magazines (particularly of animals). Place a piece of colored paper under the picture and trace the contours carefully and heavily with a pen. The tracing should leave a visible scoring of the contour on the colored paper. This can be cut out and glued to the white paper in a composition that appears to be the animal's habitat.

4. Mount the results on colored paper that matches or complements the dominant color of the composition. Other teachers and students will be awed by the startling beauty and creativity.

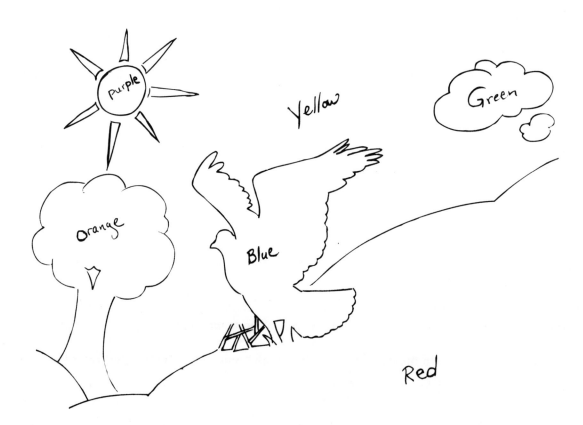

Diving into the Waters

Whether children are raised near the ocean or in a landlocked area miles from the nearest shore, the concept of oceans and seas is important for several reasons. First, the development of concepts related to oceans and seas is necessary for reading comprehension. A reader can only comprehend to the extent that he or she has experience with the concepts in a book. Naturally, children who possess no knowledge of the sea will be unable to understand and remember literature or content materials that deal with it, such as *The Cay, Call It Courage,* or *Island of the Blue Dolphins* to name only a few. Second, for science, the sea is an ecosystem of great importance. Not only is two-thirds of the Earth's water found in the seas, but many important animals live there. Furthermore, it's one of the only remaining earthbound frontiers of science.

Science experiments serve well as introductory activities for many themes. "Under the Sea" is certainly one of them. Among the science activities is one designed particularly for introducing the theme and extending children's concept knowledge. It is an activity that encourages children to look closely at fish, perhaps for the first time. You may wish to begin with this activity, or with one of the many wonderful books about the sea, the beach, or an island.

Bon voyage!

Bulletin Board Idea

 # Bibliography

Cole, J. *The Magic School Bus on the Ocean Floor.* **New York: Scholastic, 1992 (46 pages).** Ms. Frizzle's class boards the bus again for another magical field trip. They see all the wonders that await them under the sea.

Doubilet, A. *Under the Sea from A to Z.* **New York: Crown, 1991 (32 pages).** Photos and text reveal some of the more exotic animals that the ocean has to offer.

Fine, J. C. *Creatures of the Sea.* **New York: Atheneum, 1989 (31 pages).** This "fine" book introduces children to the special adaptations that allow underwater creatures to live comfortably in their surroundings.

Gelman, R. G. *Monsters of the Sea.* **Boston: Little, Brown and Co., 1990 (32 pages).** Liberal illustrations and brief text reveal to children many of the giant sea creatures of the present and the past.

Hirschi, R. *Ocean.* **New York: Bantam Books, 1991 (32 pages).** Ocean animals describe themselves and the reader is asked to guess who they might be.

Hulme, J. N. *Sea Squares.* **New York: Hyperion Books for Children, 1991 (unpaged).** Rhyming text and beautiful illustrations of ocean animals such as the whale, the sea gull, the seal and various fish. Provides opportunities to practice counting and introduces, no kidding, squaring to young readers.

Ipcar, D. Z. *Deep Sea Farm.* **New York: Alfred Knopf, 1961 (36 pages).** A kindly man with a fish's tail runs an undersea farm where he cares for fish that he frees from fishing nets and traps.

Lionni, L. *Fish Is Fish.* **New York: Pantheon, 1970 (32 pages).** A tadpole and a fish are friends, but what happens when the tadpole becomes a frog and leaves the pond? Inspires a discussion of the life of a frog.

Lionni, L. *Swimmy.* **New York: Pantheon, 1963 (31 pages).** A fish story by the torn-paper artist who brought us *Frederick* and *Fish Is Fish* (see preceding entry).

Littledale, F. *The Little Mermaid.* **New York: Scholastic, 1986 (36 pages).** A retelling of the classic Hans Christian Andersen tale of a mermaid who trades her tail for legs to win the love of a prince.

Margolis, R. J. *Wish Again, Big Bear.* **New York: Macmillan, 1972 (34 pages).** Big Bear catches a clever fish who talks his way out of being eaten by promising to grant three wishes.

McDonald, G. *The Little Island.* **New York: Dell Yearling, 1946, 1993 (36 pages).** The 1946 Caldecott winner features lavish art and a whimsical tale of a cat who learns about life and living on an island.

McGovern, A. *The Desert Beneath the Sea.* **New York: Scholastic, 1991 (48 pages).** A unique look at the animals that live under the sea through the eyes of a scientist on an undersea expedition.

Pallotta, J. *Ocean Alphabet Book.* **Watertown, MA: Charlesbridge, 1986 (32 pages).** Explore the North Atlantic from A to Z with the fish and birds that live there.

Patch, E. M. *Holiday Shore.* **New York: Macmillan, 1935 (150 pages).** The seashore's biology and marine life from the perspective of the beach.

Pfister, M. *The Rainbow Fish.* **New York: North-South Books, 1992 (unpaged).** A fish with startling beauty learns a valuable lesson about vanity and friendship.

Selsam, M. E. *See Through the Sea.* **New York: Harper, 1955 (48 pages).** From the water's edge to the ocean floor, an exploration of the animals that live at different levels beneath the sea. An oldie, but a goldie.

Straker, J. A. *Animals That Live in the Sea.* **Washington, D.C.: National Geographic Society, 1978 (31 pages).** Introduces children to the creatures that live beneath the waves and the environment they need in order to thrive.

Treherne, K. T. *The Little Mermaid.* **San Diego: Harcourt Brace Jovanovich, 1989 (unpaged).** A retelling of the classic Hans Christian Andersen tale of a mermaid who trades her tail for legs to win the love of a prince. (Also see a previous entry for the same story.)

Waters, J. F. *Giant Sea Creatures, Real and Fantastic.* **Chicago: Follett, 1973 (128 pages).** The giant creatures of myth and of reality (which are often even more fantastic) that live beneath the sea. Their habits, environment, and anatomy.

Wetterer, M. K. *The Mermaid's Cape.* **New York: Atheneum, 1981 (32 pages).** An Irish fisherman falls in love with a beautiful mermaid and steals her cape knowing that as long as he has it, she can never leave him.

Yorinks, A. *Louis the Fish.* **New York: Farrar, Strauss and Giroux, 1980 (32 pages).** A Flatbush butcher is very unhappy, but then things change for the better.

BOOKS I'VE READ ABOUT OCEANS AND SEAS

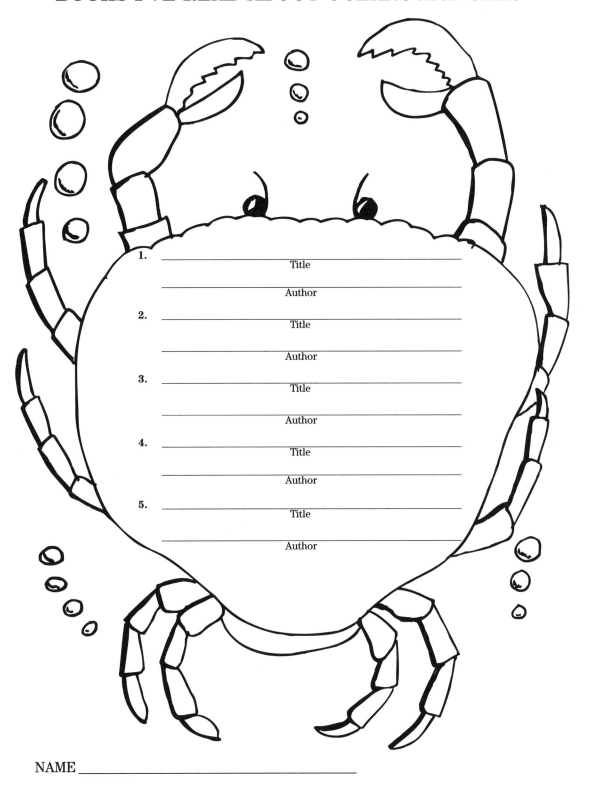

1. _____
   Title
   _____
   Author
2. _____
   Title
   _____
   Author
3. _____
   Title
   _____
   Author
4. _____
   Title
   _____
   Author
5. _____
   Title
   _____
   Author

NAME _____

The Fisherman Under the Sea
by Miyoko Matsuani

NAME _____

Directions:

Compare the story of Taro with the story of *Jack and the Beanstalk.*

1. How are the stories ALIKE?

   a. _____

   b. _____

   c. _____

2. How are the stories DIFFERENT?

   a. _____

   b. _____

   c. _____

3. Name another story in which a person travels to a strange, magical place.
   _____

4. How is this story LIKE *The Fisherman Under the Sea*?
   _____
   _____

5. How is this story DIFFERENT from *The Fisherman Under the Sea*?
   _____
   _____

The Cat Who Loved the Sea
by Rhoda Goldstein

NAME _____

Directions:

Help Hubert find his way back to the sea.

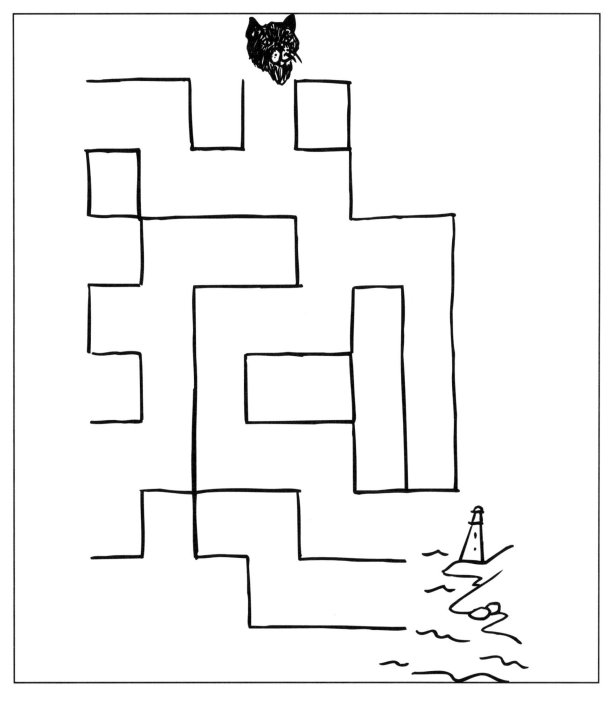

Fish Is Fish
by
Leo Leonni

NAME _____

Directions:

The pictures at the bottom of this page show how tadpoles grow into frogs. Cut out the pictures and put them in order on the "Life Cycle Wheel."

LIFE CYCLE WHEEL

1

2

3

4

5

6

© 1995 by The Center for Applied Research in Education

258

Reading

NAME _____

An Undersea Wordsearch

Directions:

Write an undersea word for each letter below. The first one is done to help you get started.

TUR **T** LE

R

E

A

S

U

R

E

Language Arts

NAME_____

What's the Story?

Directions:

Pick one of the following ideas to write about, or make up your own idea. Write a story on the back of this sheet about the idea you have chosen.

One day in the life of a SHARK!

Fish and Seagull are best friends. What would they say to each other?

You are going to sea with a famous explorer. What job would you be able to do? Where in the world would you want to go?

Invent something to help the people who fish on the oceans.

© 1995 by The Center for Applied Research in Education

Language Arts

NAME _____

Find the Adjectives

Directions:

Find the ten adjectives below and circle them.

horse	know	beautiful
submarine	starfish	skinny
April	tiny	candy
peaceful	choppy	smooth
thick	zipper	whale
huge	runner	walk
vast	eels	blue

Now write the seven adjectives that could describe the sea.

HINT:

The correct adjectives will make sense in this sentence:

I love the _____ **sea.**

_____   _____

_____   _____

_____

NAME _____

Sink or Float?

Directions:

Your teacher will give you some items. Try to guess whether each item will sink in the bucket or float on top of the water. After you have made your guesses, test each item by placing it in the water. Were your guesses correct?

ITEM	I THINK IT WILL . . .	WHEN I TESTED IT . . .
APPLE		
JAR LID		
TENNIS BALL		
PENCIL		
COIN		
NAIL		
SAFETY PIN		
PAPER CLIP		
SPOON		

© 1995 by The Center for Applied Research in Education

Fishy Things
(a teacher-led activity)

Purpose:

Use this activity to introduce the theme and to spark interest.

Materials:

8 pint jars

8 goldfish

Cardboard box

Water

Procedure:

1. Fill the jars with water and let them sit overnight to reduce the chlorine level.

2. Place the fish in the jars and keep them out of sight of the children.

3. Put the fish jars in the cardboard box, which you may want to decorate and label "MYSTERY ANIMAL."

4. On the first day of the unit, bring the box out and play 20 questions. The children ask questions. You may answer only "Yes" or "No."

5. If the children have not guessed after 20 questions, refresh their memory about the information they have and invite them to brainstorm as to what the mystery animal might be.

6. Take a jar out of the box and show the mystery animal. Ask the class how much they know about fish.

7. Divide the class into eight groups and give each group a fish jar. Encourage them to look deeply and to find and record all the information they can about fish, based on the one in the jar.

8. Move around from group to group and encourage with questions such as "How does it move?" "How does it breathe?" "Why is it doing that?" "Do you know what fish eat?"

9. When it appears that the groups have exhausted their available knowledge, "jigsaw" by having each group in turn contribute one characteristic of fish to a master list.

10. Distribute the page "Fishy Things" and have students identify, alone or in groups, the characteristics from that master list that are true of all or most fish.

11. If you can, put the fish in a common bowl, aquarium, or container. It's nice to have them present for the duration of the theme. Include marbles, colored sand, and aquarium decor. If you'd rather not become a fish breeder, it's nice to offer them to children when the theme is over. Get parental permission in writing.

NOTE: It is possible (and somewhat easier) to do this without the fish jars, but it's not as effective. Having the fish present inspires and encourages the children's thinking about fish. Besides it's more fun and more engaging to have the fish there.

NAME_____

Fishy Things

Directions:

After the class names all the characteristics about fish, use the list to complete this page.

List characteristics that are true of all fish:

_____
_____
_____
_____
_____
_____

List characteristics that are true of some fish, but not all:

_____
_____
_____
_____
_____

List anything you can think of that is not true of any fish:

_____
_____
_____
_____
_____

Growing Brine Shrimp
(a teacher-led activity)

Concepts:

Small sea animals come from eggs. Sea water is salty.

Materials:

Brine shrimp eggs (available as fish food from any pet store)

Large glass jar or small aquarium

Non-iodized Kosher salt

Distilled water or aged tap water

Eye droppers

Procedure:
(If you prefer all measurements can be cut in half.)

1. If you are using tap water, obtain 2 quarts and allow it to sit undisturbed and uncovered for 48 hours to reduce the chlorine level.

2. Place 5 teaspoons of non-iodized Kosher salt (do not use common table salt) in the prepared water and stir for a few minutes to dissolve it.

3. Introduce 1/2 teaspoon of brine shrimp eggs to the water.

4. Place this "brine shrimp incubator" in a warm place.

5. Each day, obtain a drop of water and view it under the microscope. Children will respond with real excitement when, in about two days, little, multi-legged "swimmers" are seen.

6. Encourage children to draw the little animals.

7. Continue to check a drop each day and record how the little swimmers grow and change.

8. If you have classroom fish (a good idea if you are studying the sea) you might want to use the brine shrimp to show children how the undersea food chain and survival adaptations work. Simply introduce some brine shrimp eggs into the fish tank or, if you have saltwater fish, introduce the fish into the brine shrimp environment. Explain that brine shrimp lay millions of eggs, and many are eaten by fish. Many survive and hatch but many of those are eaten by fish before they can lay eggs of their own. A few, however, will survive and lay millions of eggs each. How does this adaptation help brine shrimp survive as a species? Many small animals have this characteristic of sheer numbers as their major hedge against extinction. Think of various kinds of insects like ants, mosquitoes, and gnats. Perhaps children can find other water animals that have this characteristic.

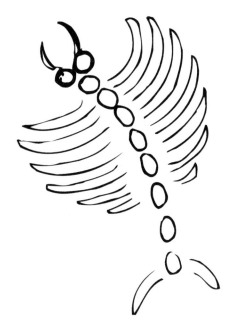
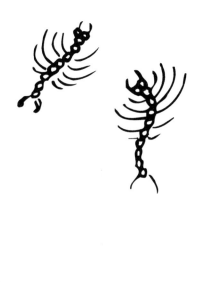

NAME _____

Undersea Pictures

Directions:

The undersea pictures below can be divided exactly in half. Draw a line to show how the pictures can be divided. This is called a "line of symmetry." The first one is done for you.

268 Math

Submerged Subtraction

Directions:

Use your arithmetic skills to solve the problems below.

```
  9      7      6      8      9
 -2     -3     -4     -3     -5
 ___    ___    ___    ___    ___
```

```
  5             6      7      8
 -2            -3     -5     -2
 ___           ___    ___    ___
```

NAME _____

Solve the Problems

Directions:

Use your arithmetic skills to solve the problems below.

NAME_____

Help the Pirate

Howdy, you land lovers! I need you to help me. I'm not very good at math, you see. Please help me by correcting these problems.

NAME _____

Let's Read the Map

Directions:

Many people make a living from the sea. The map below is the island of Goldenland. Use the map to answer the questions below.

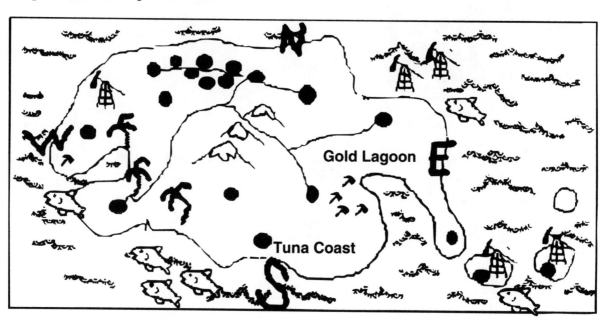

1. Each dot is a town. Which part of the island (N, S, E, or W) has the most people? _____

2. Each fish represents a good fishing area. Which part of the island (N, S, E, or W) has the best fishing? _____

3. A bay is like a lake except that it is part of the sea and has land on three sides. Find a bay and label it with a B.

4. Each hammer shows where a gold mine is located. How many gold mines are on the island of Goldenland? _____

5. Each tower shows where an oil well is located. Which part of the island (N, S, E, or W) has the most wells? _____

NAME_____

Which State?

Directions:

Can you think of a state near the sea that fits each description? Choose from the states in the box below.

1. I am north of Cuba. Oranges grow here. _____

2. I am near a gulf and the Mississippi River flows through me to the sea.
   _____

3. The Pacific Ocean washes up on my long shoreline. Oranges grow here and many movies are made here. _____

4. I am close to Russia. Whales, seals, and many kinds of fish are found in my North Pacific waters. _____

5. One of my cities has the same name as me. Manhattan Island is part of me and many ships that come to the United States stop at one of my piers.
   _____

6. I am a group of islands in the South Pacific Ocean. One of my products is pearls which grow in oyster shells. _____

7. I am just south of Canada and my coastline is on the North Pacific Ocean.
   _____

8. I am just south of Washington, D.C. and my coastline is on the Atlantic Ocean.
   _____

California	Louisiana	North Carolina
Alaska	Nevada	Washington
Minnesota	Hawaii	Florida
Virginia	New York	Utah
	Ohio	

Social Studies

A "Fishy" Scene
(a teacher-led activity)

Materials:

Variety of colored tissue paper

Pencils and markers

White drawing paper

Paintbrushes

Liquid starch

Plastic bowls like those in which whipped margarine is sold

Template pattern

File folders or tagboard

Directions:

1. Make templates of the oval on file folders or tagboard.

2. Using a pencil, lightly trace the outline of the oval onto the white paper.

3. With the oval as the fish body, lightly add top and bottom fins, a round eye, and a fan-shaped tail.

4. Lightly add a line to make a sandy sea bed and include plants or other sea-like features as the muse strikes you.

5. Tear colored tissue into small, roughly circular pieces.

6. Lay pieces of tissue on sections of the light line drawing and paint them down with liquid starch. The colors will run together to suggest an undersea view.

7. Continue until the entire line drawing is "painted." Then outline the color areas with felt pens to dress up the edges.

8. Frames or mounts made of construction paper will also help to "finish" the works.

TEMPLATE PATTERN FOR "A FISHY SCENE"

Stop the Destruction

Protecting our Earth and its resources is something with which your students can help. Here are some activities to help you introduce this new theme.

Explain the Problem. Junk mail is often thrown out without being read or used in any way. This mountain of paper is sent to landfills where it sits for years before decomposing. One family can receive 25 to 30 pieces of junk mail a week!

Do the Math. Show the children the extent of the problem by writing "25 pieces" on the board. A town with only 9,000 citizens has about 3,000 households. Write "3,000 families" on the board. Multiply 25 (pieces) times 3,000 (families) and show the result of 75,000 pieces of junk mail for a small town each week.

Get a Sense of the Problem. Invite children to bring their families' junk mail for one week (a parent letter is included in this theme). At the end of the week, spread the collected junk mail on a table or on the floor. Open any still-sealed envelopes. Remove and separate the contents into piles (i.e., envelopes, cards, sheets). This should give children a firm grasp of the extent of the junk-mail problem in landfills.

Separate the Trash. Place the recyclable paper (non-glossy) in a box for recycling. Dispose of the non-recyclable materials.

Do Something About It! Distribute three to five copies of the notice below to each student. Explain that this can be enclosed in the return envelopes that usually come with junk mail to ask companies to stop sending unwanted and wasteful paper to the students' homes.

Family name_____

Address_____

City_____ State_____ Zip_____

To whom it may concern:

    In an effort to reduce our disposable waste products, our family requests that you remove our name from your mailing list.

    Thank you.

        The _____ Family

Dear Parent or Guardian:

Our class is studying ecology and ways that we can make the Earth a cleaner place while preserving our resources. One of our activities will be to collect junk mail from each family for one week. We want to see how much waste paper is put into landfills each week from junk mail. Please save your unwanted junk mail for us and send it to school with your child. We will dispose of it properly when we are done and recycle whatever we can.

Teacher_____

Your son/daughter_____

···

Querido Padres:

En clase estamos estudiando ecologia. Estamos aprendiendo diferentes formas de limpar nuestra Tierra y de proteger nuestros recursos naturales. Una de nuestras actividades es colectar el "correo basura" que le llega a cada familia durante una semana. Queremos saber cuanto papel de "correo basura" de desperdicio es despositado semanalmente en los tiraderos municipales.

Por favor, guarde su "correo basura" por esta semana y mandenoslo ala escuela con su hijo(a). Nosotros lo desecharemos adecuadamente y reciclaremos cuanto sea posible una vez terminado el estudio.

Maestra(o)_____

Su Hija(o)_____

Bibliography

Baker, J. *Where the Forest Meets the Sea*. New York: Greenwillow Books, 1987 (32 pages). During a camping trip in the Australian rainforest, a boy wonders what the future holds for the rich and varied plant and animal life around him.

Carlson, L. *EcoArt!: Earth-Friendly Arts & Crafts for 3- to 9-year olds*. Charlotte, VT: Williamson Publishing, 1992 (154 pages). Many fun, engaging and useful art projects that treat the Earth kindly.

Cherry, L. *The Great Kapok Tree*. San Diego: Harcourt Brace Jovanovich, 1990 (32 pages). The animals that live in a huge kapok tree in the Amazon rainforest come to a man as he sleeps and plead with him not to cut the tree down.

Cowcher, H. *El Bosque Tropical (The Rain Forest)*. New York: Scholastic, 1992 (34 pages). The animals of the rainforest live in peace and harmony, fearing only the jaguar, until a creature even more frightening disrupts their forest home. English and Spanish versions available.

DePaola, T. *Michael Bird-boy*. Englewood Cliffs, NJ: Prentice Hall Books for Young Readers, 1975 (32 pages). A young boy who loves his land must find the source of the black clouds that hang over it.

Foreman, M. *Dinosaurs and All That Rubbish*. New York: Crowell, 1973 (32 pages). After ruining the Earth, the man leaves for another planet. When he returns years later and finds that animals have returned the Earth to its former beauty, he decides to stay. Will the animals welcome him back?

Gibbons, G. *Recycle!: A Handbook for Kids*. Boston: Little, Brown & Co., 1992 (unpaged). Shows children what happens to glass, paper, aluminum, and other materials when they are recycled into new products.

Greene, C. *The Old Ladies Who Liked Cats*. New York: Harper Collins, 1991 (32 pages). Old ladies are told by the people of the island not to let their cats out at night. That decision spells disaster for the ecology on the tiny island.

Hailey, G. *Noah's Ark*. New York: Atheneum, 1971 (30 pages). Like the Noah of Old, this Noah builds an ark, but this one is to save the animals from a polluted world after he dreams of an empty zoo.

Leedy, L. *The Great Trash Bash*. New York: Holiday House, 1991 (32 pages). The animals that live in Beaston need to find better ways to control and recycle their trash.

Mazer, A. *The Salamander Room*. New York: Alfred Knopf, 1991 (24 pages). A boy and his mother discuss the needs of a pet salamander and find that the home should become an ecosystem.

Pearce, F. *The Big Green Book.* **New York: Grossett & Dunlap, 1988 (32 pages).** Shows how humans affect the Earth and what people need to do to save it.

Peet, B. *The Wump World.* **Boston: Houghton Mifflin, 1970 (44 pages).** The Wump World is a beautiful land until it is taken over by huge numbers of tiny creatures from the foul world of Pollutus.

Pringle, L. *The Only Earth We Have.* **New York: Macmillan, 1969 (86 pages).** Explores the causes of air, soil, and water pollution and the effects upon human and animal life.

Seuss, Dr. *The Lorax.* **New York: Random House, 1971 (70 pages).** The Onceler tells the tale of a local pollution problem.

Shanks, A. *About Garbage and Stuff.* **New York: Viking, 1973 (40 pages).** A book that is over 20 years old, but unfortunately, still has much to say about waste and recycling through text and photos.

Simons, R. *Recyclopedia: Games, Science Equipment and Crafts from Recycled Materials.* **Boston: Houghton Mifflin, 1976 (118 pages).** The title says it all!

Thompson, C. *The Paper Bag Prince.* **New York: Alfred Knopf, 1992 (unpaged).** A wise old man moves into a railroad car on the outskirts of the town dump and watches as Nature gradually reclaims the polluted field.

Weir, B. *Panther Dream: A Story of the African Rainforest.* **New York: Hyperion Books for Children, 1991 (40 pages).** A boy out hunting for food for his family meets a panther who teaches him of the intricate and delicate web of life in the rainforest.

Wildsmith, B. *Professor Noah's Spaceship.* **New York: Oxford University Press, 1980 (30 pages).** When the birds and animals are no longer happy in their ruined forest homes, Professor Noah takes them away in his amazing spaceship. But where will they go?

Willow, D. *At Home in the Rainforest.* **Watertown, MA: Charlesbridge, 1991 (30 pages).** An introduction to the abundant life forms in an Amazon rainforest.

NAME _____

ECOLOGY BOOKS I'VE READ

1. _____
   Title
   _____
   Author
2. _____
   Title
   _____
   Author
3. _____
   Title
   _____
   Author
4. _____
   Title
   _____
   Author
5. _____
   Title
   _____
   Author

© 1995 by The Center for Applied Research in Education

The Paper Bag Prince
by
Colin Thompson

NAME _____

Directions:

To reduce the amount of trash that schools throw into landfills, the President has asked you to invent a **NO-WASTE SACK LUNCH**.

> A sack lunch with a sandwich, a juice drink, some chips, cookies and an apple makes a LOT of waste. There's the paper lunch bag, the plastic wrap for the sandwich, the plastic wrap for the cookies, and the empty juice box. Can you design a lunch with NO WASTE?

1. What will you carry it in? _____

    Will this   REDUCE   REUSE   or   RECYCLE?

2. What will you put the sandwich in to keep it fresh? _____
_____

    Will this   REDUCE   REUSE   or   RECYCLE?

3. What will you put the cookies in to keep them fresh? _____
_____

    Will this   REDUCE   REUSE   or   RECYCLE?

4. What kind of container can hold the juice? _____
_____

    Will this   REDUCE   REUSE   or   RECYCLE?

DRAW A PICTURE OF YOUR NO-WASTE LUNCH ON THE BACK OF THIS PAGE.

The Great Kapok Tree
by Lynne Cherry

NAME _____

Directions:

After reading *The Great Kapok Tree*, read and answer the questions below. Think carefully about your answers.

1. The animals gently asked the man not to chop down the tree. What would YOU say to him?

   _____
   _____
   _____

2. Can you name three animals in your country that live in woods or forests?

   _____
   _____

3. What would happen to the animals if the trees and forests were gone?

   _____
   _____

4. Can you name other bad things that would happen if the forests and woods were gone?

   _____
   _____

5. What are some things you can do to keep the woods and forests from being destroyed?

   _____
   _____

The Salamander Room
by Anne Mazer

NAME _____

Directions:
Choose an animal that most people would not think of as a pet. Answer the questions below as Brian answered his mother's questions in *The Salamander Room*.

1. What kind of animal did you choose? _____

2. Where will it sleep? _____
   _____

3. When it wakes up, where will it play? _____
   _____

4. It will miss its friends in the forest. What can you do? _____
   _____

5. It will be hungry. How will you feed it? _____
   _____

6. And you—where will you sleep? _____
   _____

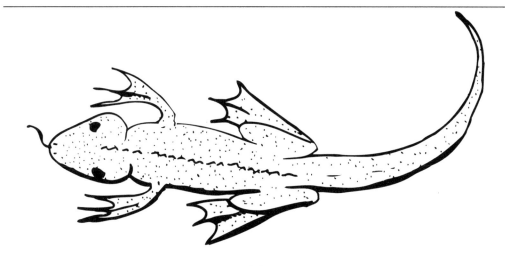

Poetry from Trash!
(a teacher-led activity)

Before beginning, explain to the children that they will be writing a poem. Explain the "blank verse" and read the example below. Then explain the procedure.

Step 1: Clip interesting words from magazine ads and article titles.

Step 2: Put the strips in a box or large manila envelope.

Step 3: Arrange the children into pairs or trios.

Step 4: Have one child in each group take a pinchful of strips.

Step 5: Use the strips as the foundation of a blank verse poem. Let the word strip suggest a topic.

Step 6: Use a process approach to write and publish the poems. They usually solicit awe from readers who don't know how they were created.

Example:

> *Given the words:*
> blast, risk, hunting down, corners, beasts, brain, safety

My brain was once a place of safety.

Now it is filled with risk.

I must begin hunting down

The beasts in the corners of my mind

and blast them from the shadows. —*A Fifth-Grade Boy*

State Your Case!

Directions:

Think of a product that has more packaging than it needs to have. Use the space below to plan a letter to the company that makes it. Your letter should explain two things: (1) why you think the product has too much packaging and (2) what the company can do that would be better.

1. Why the product has too much packaging . . .

   _____
   _____
   _____
   _____

2. What the company can do that would be better . . .

   _____
   _____
   _____
   _____
   _____
   _____
   _____

NAME _____

What I Think About Ecology

Directions:

Think about the statements below. Finish them using your own ideas.

1. The rainforest is important because _____
   _____

2. The most important thing to recycle is _____ because
   _____

3. If I could change one thing about the way people treat the environment, I'd want to change
   _____
   _____

4. The easiest way for me to REDUCE is _____ because
   _____

5. The easiest way for me to REUSE is _____ because
   _____

© 1995 by The Center for Applied Research in Education

Language Arts

We Care About the Earth
(a teacher-led activity)

Objective:
Integrate writing, reading, and oral language

Materials:
Writing materials, media equipment, and examples of Public Service Announcements (PSAs). Ideally, the work should be videotaped, but if this is not possible, photographic slides with audio recordings will serve nicely. "Radio Ads" using only cassette tape is also an alternative. Your local radio station has PSAs and will be glad to make copies for you if you bring a tape. You can videotape examples of PSAs on late night television, if you choose to do so.

Procedure:

1. *Divide the class into groups.* Three to six children per group, depending on the children's talents and the size of the project.

2. *Model.* Allow children to listen to or watch a PSA as a model for the activity they will engage in.

3. *Brainstorm.* What messages does the public need to hear about REDUCING, REUSING, and RECYCLING and protecting wildlife? What are some slogans (such as "Don't Throw It All Away" or "Put Litter in Its Place") that can be used?

4. *Write.* Each group creates a "spot" (as broadcasters call them) with a statement of the problem, a suggestion, and a slogan. A writer's workshop approach with peer conferences to refine and organize is highly recommended.

5. *"Publish."* Videotape or otherwise record the spot. The group may want to choose their best reader or "turn-read" in which each member takes a portion. The recorded "spots" can be shared with other classes and make great presentations at the PTA, PTO, Home-School Association or open house.

The Balance of Nature

"Balance of nature" refers to the way nature keeps everything in balance. Read this story and think about it. Then tell what you think below.

Town Without Wolves

Near the town of Foothills, there used to be many wolves. The people of the town knew that the wolves killed and ate deer. "The deer are so pretty," the people said. "We don't want those mean wolves to kill them!"

The people of the town went into the hills to get rid of the wolves. Some hunted and others trapped. Soon the wolves were all gone. The people of Foothills were happy because all the wolves were gone.

One morning, the Mayor of Foothills woke up early and went out to get the newspaper. Out in the yard she saw a large deer, eating from her trashcan. "Oh, you are so pretty!" she said. But then another deer came and another and another. They trampled her garden and knocked over her trashcans.

"Get away!" she yelled, and the deer ran off into the hills. The mayor went into her house. The phone was ringing.

"Hello?"

"Mayor, there are three deer in my garden! What shall I do?" the caller said.

"There were deer in my yard too," said the Mayor. "Scare them away."

Very soon the phone rang again. Then again and again. People all over town were complaining about deer in their yards, in the streets and in the alleys eating from trashcans.

"What can we do?" they asked the Mayor.

1. Why do you think there were so many deer? _____

   _____

2. Why do you think the deer came into town? _____

3. What are some problems that can be caused by having deer in people's yards and in the

   streets. _____

   _____

4. How was the balance of nature put "out of balance" in this story? _____

_____

_____

5. If the people of Foothills learn about the balance of nature, what might they do to get the deer population back to normal (besides shooting them)? Write your answer on the back of this sheet.

NAME _____

Animals in the Wild

Directions:

The three animals on this page are best suited to certain kinds of environments. Circle the environment you think is better for each animal and explain why on the back of this page.

Organic Material
(a teacher-led activity)

Purpose:

Children will learn about the forces that break organic materials down to a state that can join with soil.

Materials:

Five sealable food storage bags

Five adhesive labels

A small amount of fresh fertile soil

A small amount of fresh water

Five equal portions of common organic materials (such as apple, bread, banana peel, or some other)

Procedure:

1. Divide into five groups. Label groups: Air, Darkness, Earth, Light, Water.

2. Put the organic material in the bag.

3. "Air" group should add plenty of air and then seal the bag.

4. "Darkness" group should remove the air, seal the bag, and store it in a dark place.

5. "Earth" group should add enough fresh fertile soil to cover the material, remove the air, and then seal the bag.

6. "Light" group should remove the air, seal the bag, and then store it in a well-lit place.

7. "Water" group should add enough water to cover the material, remove the air, and then seal the bag.

8. ALL bags are stored in the darkness except the "Light" group's bag.

9. After 7 days have passed, each group should look at its bag (EXPLAIN THAT THEY MUST NOT OPEN THEM), observe the changes, and then collaborate on a scientific journaling of the observation. How has it changed? Predict the state of the organic material in a week; two weeks.

10. After 14 days students should observe, journal, and predict again.

11. After 21 days students should observe, journal, and illustrate the steps in the decomposing process using the "Observation Sheet."

12. Post the five groups' Observation Sheets for easy comparison. Which variable had the greatest effect on the organic materials? What two variables—Air/Darkness; Light/Dirt; Dirt/Water, etc.—will help organic garbage break down the fastest?

13. Extend learning. Have children write a letter to their state congressional representative describing this experiment and explaining how to return organic waste to the Earth most efficiently. The class may collaborate, or children can write their own. These should be sent and children can expect a letter of response.

NAME _____

Organic Material Observation Sheet

Directions:

In the boxes below, draw or describe the changes you observed in the materials in your bag.

One Week

Two Weeks

Three Weeks

NAME_____

Math Problems to Solve

Directions:

Each story has a math problem. Check the "Fact Box" to find the problem. Write it in the box next to the story.

1. Jaime collected 38 aluminum cans and Raoul collected 37 aluminum cans. When they were finished, they had 75 cans.

2. Andrea collected 17 bundles of newspapers last week. She collected 4 on Monday, 6 on Tuesday, 3 on Wednesday, and 4 on Friday.

3. Mr. Locken's class agreed to drink juice from aluminum cans instead of boxes at lunchtime. In three days they reduced waste by 53 juice boxes. 15 kids bought juice cans on Monday. 18 bought juice cans on Tuesday. 20 bought juice cans on Wednesday.

4. Heather, Andy, Julia, Maria, and Donny decided to save gasoline by helping their parents set up a Share-a-Ride for daily rides to school. They saved 10 gallons each day for 5 days. They saved 50 gallons of gas all together.

5. Michael used to replace the six batteries in his boombox every two months. Since he started using rechargeable batteries four months ago, he has saved 12 batteries.

   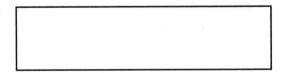

Fact Box

6 × 2 = 12	15 + 18 + 20 = 53	10 × 5 = 50
38 + 37 = 75	4 + 6 + 3 + 4 = 17	

© 1995 by The Center for Applied Research in Education

Complete the Multiplication Table

Directions:

Finish this table by multiplying the top numbers with the side numbers. Write the answer in the box where the columns and rows meet. 5 x 5 is done for you.

X	1	2	3	4	5	6	7	8	9	10
1										
2										
3										
4										
5					25					
6										
7										
8										
9										
10										

NAME_____

Light the Bulbs

Directions:

Your brain is the only power I need to light the bulbs below. Color the bulb yellow if you think the statement is true. Color it brown if you think it is false.

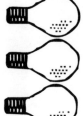

1. Rainforests are homes for many kinds of animals.

2. There are lots of ways to recycle.

3. We can cut down all the trees we want.

4. When we go on picnics we can REDUCE by using plastic forks instead of real forks.

5. When we buy soda, we can RECYCLE our cans.

6. One way to REUSE is to buy batteries that can be recharged.

7. More waste comes from cities than from small towns.

8. Only certain people can help the environment by reducing waste.

9. Only adults can help the environment by recycling.

10. Only the land and the water can be polluted.

Choose one false statement above and explain why it is false.

_____

_____

Climb the Kapok Tree

Directions:

Climb the kapok tree! Use the words from the box below to complete this puzzle and to climb the tree.

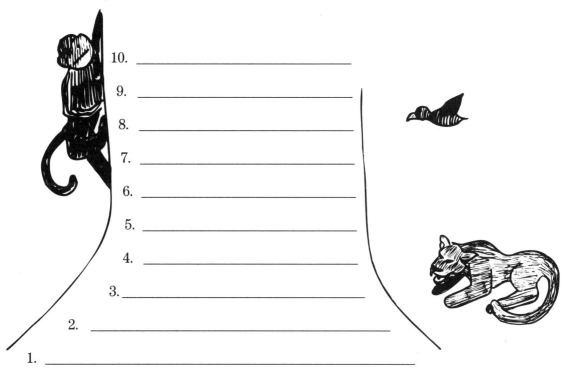

10. A country on the continent of South America.

9. The name for the climate near the Equator.

8. The rainforest is in a hot and damp _____.

7. Monkey see, _____ do.

6. Like Kermit, but they don't live in a swamp.

5. Lots of trees but it's not a forest.

4. A bird that "talks"

3. Animals that are almost extinct.

2. Kapok trees grow in the tropical _____.

1. The continent with the world's largest rainforest.

jungle	Tree frog	Brazil
parrot	tropical	rainforest
endangered	monkey	South America
climate		

NAME _____

Which Package Is Better?

Directions:

Look at each kind of product below. Decide which package is BEST for the environment and circle it.

	tube with box	pump
Toothpaste	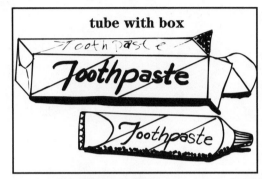	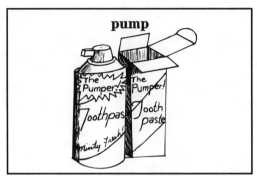
	big box	variety pack
Cereal		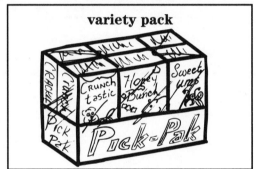
	fresh	frozen
Vegetables		
	mix packet	6 plastic bottles
Fruit Drink		

Recycle Those Egg Cartons

Materials:

Egg cartons; other art materials to cut and decorate such as glue, scissors, construction paper, pipe cleaners, fabric, yard, buttons, googly eyes, and so forth.

Procedure:

Cut away egg cups and use your imagination to fashion them into animals. Here are four examples.

Global Carnival

Sharing, Speaking, Listening

Dedicating certain days to certain aspects of a theme adds much to the aura of festivity and excitement. Here are four activities that provide opportunities for sharing, speaking, and listening.

EAT-THE-WORLD DAY: Set one day aside for children to bring foods from other cultures and other lands. These can be common, such as tortilla chips, fortune cookies, and canoles, or may be more exotic such as sopopillas, goat's milk, and shrimp etufe. Children should bring enough to share with ten people. Each child explains what he or she brought, how it is made, and any other interesting thing about it. Then, the item is set out for sampling. In a class of 25, there will be 250 servings, so naturally not everyone can eat everything.

WEAR-THE-WORLD DAY: On this day each student will wear an article of clothing from another land, is similar in style to something worn in another land, or that celebrates another land or culture. Articles of clothing may range from a "Free South Africa" T-shirt to a poncho made in Equador to a sarape from the Far East. Each child shares with the group what the article of clothing is, where it is from, and how it is worn.

BRING-THE-WORLD DAY: On this day children bring any item they have from another land, excluding clothing. Items range from foreign coins to tourist souvenirs to family heirlooms. Once again, the child explains the item, where it is from, and how it was acquired.

READ-THE-WORLD DAY: Each child reads a folktale from another culture or tradition and shares it with the class. Several sentences telling what the story is about and inviting others to read it is usually sufficient. Older children can write the stories in their own words, crafting them in the folktale style, and final versions can be bound into a book "Folktales from Around the World."

Bulletin Board Idea

Bibliography

Aardema, V. *Bringing the Rain to Kapiti Plain.* **New York: Dial Press, 1981 (32 pages).** Delightful rhyme in the tradition of "The House That Jack Built," which tells how Ki-Pat ended the drought on the African Plain.

Baker, K. *The Magic Fan.* **San Diego: Harcourt Brace Jovanovich, 1989 (20 pages).** Yoshi, a master carpenter, builds a boat to catch the moon, a kite to reach the clouds and a rainbow bridge while his neighbors snicker and jeer.

De Paola, T. *The Legend of the Bluebonnet.* **New York: Putnam, 1983 (30 pages).** A retelling of the old Comanche legend of how a girl's sacrifice brought the bluebonnet flower to the Texas prairie.

De Paola, T. *The Legend of the Indian Paintbrush.* **New York: Putnam, 1988 (40 pages).** A retelling of the Indian legend in which Little Gopher, an artist for his people, brings the colors of the sunset to Earth.

Friedman, I. *How My Parents Learned to Eat.* **Boston: Houghton Mifflin, 1984 (30 pages).** A young American sailor and his Japanese girlfriend secretly learn each other's way of eating.

Golenbock, P. *Teammates.* **San Diego: Harcourt Brace Jovanovich, 1991 (29 pages).** A tender story of the true-life friendship between PeeWee Reese and Jackie Robinson, the first African-American in Major League Baseball.

Hidaka, M. *Girl from the Snow Country.* **New York: Kane/Miller Books, 1986 (31 pages).** A little Japanese girl makes snow bunnies as she walks across a snowy field to market with her mother.

Johnson, R. *Kenji and the Magic Geese.* **New York: Simon & Schuster Books for Young Readers, 1992 (unpaged).** A goose in a painting on Kenji's wall flies away to join a flock of wild geese.

Joseph, L. *Coconut Kind of Day: Island Poems.* **New York: Puffin, 1990 (unpaged).** A collection of poetry that explores the life of children of the Caribbean Islands. Melodic verse and lavish art.

Kalman, M. *Sayonara, Mrs. Kackleman.* **New York: Viking Kestrel, 1989 (34 pages).** Two American children visit Japan and learn about the culture and traditions of the people.

Kimmel, E. *Anansi Goes Fishing.* **New York: Holiday House, 1992 (28 pages).** A classic tale of trickery from the African folktale.

Lobel, A. *The Dwarf Giant.* **New York: Holiday House, 1991 (unpaged).** A rude dwarf uses dangerous games and trickery to manipulate a Japanese prince and princess.

Luen, N. *The Dragon Kite.* San Diego: Harcourt Brace Jovanovich, 1982 (32 pages). A clever thief fashions a magnificent kite to aid him in stealing a pair of golden dolphins from a castle roof.

Martin, B. *Knots on a Counting Rope.* New York: Holt, 1987 (32 pages). Strength-of-Blue-Horses, a Native American boy, reminisces with his grandfather about his birth, his first horse, and an exciting horse race.

McKissack, P. *Mirandy and Brother Wind.* New York: Alfred Knopf, 1988 (29 pages). Mirandy, an African-American in the deep South, tries to capture The Wind to help her win a dance contest.

Miles, M. *Annie and the Old One.* Boston: Little, Brown and Co., 1971 (40 pages). Annie, a Native American girl, tries to forestall her beloved grandmother's passing.

Mosel, A. *Tikki Tikki Tembo.* New York: Holt, Rinehart, Winston, 1968 (45 pages). A Chinese fable. A boy with a very long name falls in a well. Much time is spent getting help because his name is so long and hard to pronounce. This, the story suggests, is why the Chinese always give their children short names.

Osofsky, A. *Dreamcatcher.* New York: Orchard Books 1992 (unpaged) A baby sleeps among his Ojibway people, safe from bad dreams, as the life of the village goes on around him.

Say, A. *The Bicycle Man.* Boston: Houghton Mifflin, 1982 (40 pages). Two American soldiers showcase their bicycle tricks at a school sports day in occupied Japan.

Scott, A. *On Mother's Lap.* New York Clarion Books, 1992 (32 pages). A mother's lap, a young Eskimo boy learns, is a very special place with plenty of room for all.

Snyder, D. *The Boy of the Three Year Nap.* Boston: Houghton-Mifflin, 1988 (32 pages). A poor Japanese mother tricks her lazy son into changing his habits.

Taylor, M. *Mississippi Bridge.* New York: Bantam Skylark, 1990 (62 pages). A highly recommended read-aloud for children in grades 3 and up. This story of a terrible tragedy set against the backdrop of the Depression and racial prejudice is another triumph from the author of *Roll of Thunder, Hear My Cry*. Written in dialect.

Walter, M. *Brother to the Wind.* New York: Lothrop, Lee & Shepard, 1985 (32 pages). A young African boy's wishes come true with the help of a friendly snake.

Williams, K. *When Africa Was Home.* New York: Orchard Books, 1991 (30 pages). Peter's family remembers how happy they were when they lived in Africa and Peter's father vows that they will return there.

GLOBAL BOOKS I'VE READ

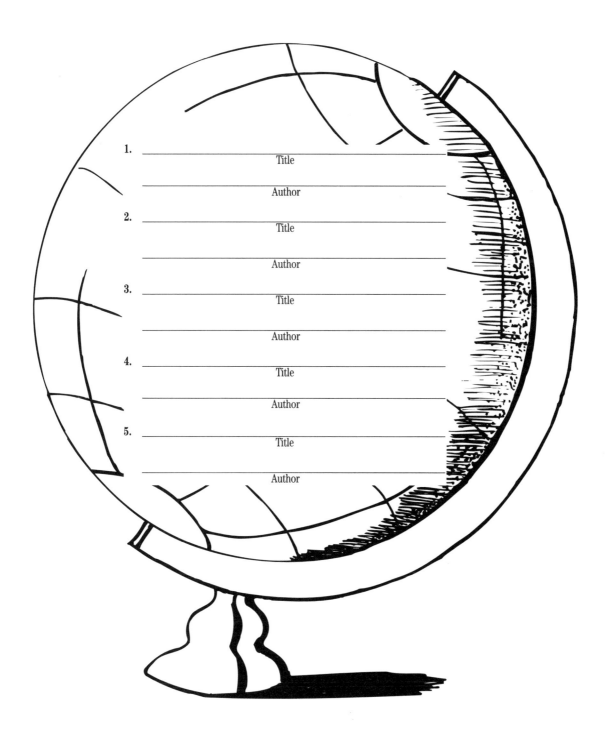

NAME _____

Teammates
by
Peter Golenbock

NAME _____

Directions:

After reading or listening to *Teammates*, complete the activities below.

1. List three ways that people mistreated Jackie Robinson.

   _____
   _____
   _____

2. Why was Jackie treated this way?

   _____
   _____
   _____

3. List three ways that people are mistreated today just because of the color of their skin.

   _____
   _____
   _____

4. Branch Rickey said, "I want a man with the courage not to fight back." What do you think he meant by this?

   _____
   _____
   _____

5. What do you think would have happened if Jackie Robinson did try to fight back?

   _____
   _____
   _____

Mississippi Bridge
by
Mildred D. Taylor

NAME _____

1. There were two persons who looked at the blue hat in Wallace's Store. Compare and contrast the treatment each person was given.

Rudine Johnson	Miz Hattie

2. Why do you think Wallace said to Rudine, "You know I can't let you try on that hat."

_____

_____

3. What do think would happen if he DID let Rudine try the hat on? _____

_____

_____

Mississippi Bridge
by
Mildred D. Taylor

NAME _____

Directions:

Pretend you are Josias. Write a letter to your cousin explaining what happened to you and how you feel about it. Remember what Josias said to Jeremy and try to make your letter have the same "voice."

Mississippi Bridge
by
Mildred D. Taylor

NAME _____

Directions:

Pretend you are Rudine. Write a letter to your friend explaining what happened to you and how you feel about it. Remember how Rudine spoke to Mr. Wallace and try to make your letter have the same "voice."

Colors
by Shel Silverstein
Where the Sidewalk Ends

NAME _____

Directions:
After reading the poem, complete the activities on this sheet.

1. This poem has both silliness and truth. What is one thing in the poem that seems impossible to you? _____

   _____

2. What is one thing that seems true to you? _____

   _____

3. Reread the last two lines. What does Shel Silverstein mean when he writes "All the colors I am inside have not been invented yet"? _____

   _____

   _____

4. INSIDE means "dreams, thoughts, feelings, and ideas" in this poem. My dreams are red because they are as sweet as fruit punch. What color are YOU inside?

My dreams are _____

My thoughts are _____

My feelings are _____

My ideas are   _____

312   Language Arts

© 1995 by The Center for Applied Research in Education

Global Carnival

A Poem for Two Voices
(a teacher-led activity)

The process for teaching this poetic form must include (a) Modeling, (b) Brainstorming, (c) Ample Writing Time, and (d) Sharing.

1. **MODELING:** Write the following poem on an overhead, butcher paper, or the chalkboard. Boys read the left, girls read the right, and everyone reads the middle. You might find it helpful helpful to color code.

We're Much the Same

We are boys.		
		We are girls.
	We are different	
	but much the same.	
We like daytime.		
		We like nighttime.
We wear black shoes.		
		We wear white shoes.
	We are all in school.	
We like reading.		
		We like math.
	But we both like lunch!	

2. **BRAINSTORMING:** Explain to the children that they will be pairing up to write just such a poem, exploring the ways they are different and the same. Ask them to suggest ways that people differ and write them on the board, overhead, or easel. Seek suggestions related to height, eye color, hair color, hobbies, numbers of children in the family, and so on. Put the written suggestions in a visible place so that they may be used as a reference while writing.

3. **TIME TO WRITE:** Children shouldn't NEED a sheet to guide the process. All they need do is identify similarities and differences and write them in a poem for two voices (like the model). However, for children who need the guidance, a format guide is provided. It is useful both for children who have difficulties with creative activities and for those who may not have been present the day of the activity, but would like to participate.

   The teaching will need to facilitate the writing as it progresses. There are always those children who believe they are finished after providing a bare minimum and others who have scarcely begun by that time. Encourage children, as they write, to work to the full extent of their capabilities.

4. **SHARING:** Writing has no purpose if it is not shared with others. If children know their work will be "published," it adds a new dimension to the authorship. A poem for two voices should be shared orally by the pair who wrote it. It is not possible to hear the true "voice of the poem" when it is read silently by a spectator. Plan a time when the poems will be shared and honor all the writers by showcasing them. A special or fancy "Author's Chair" or an ornate sign under which to stand while reading helps to formalize the proceeding.

NAME _____

NAME _____

Format Guide

Directions:

This sheet is for two people. Make a list of things that are the same and different about yourselves. Then use the list to write a poem.

My name is_____.   My name is_____.

I like_____.   I like_____.

    We both like_____.

I have_____.   I have_____.

    But we both like_____.

My hair is_____.   My hair is_____.

My family is_____.   My family is_____.

    And we both_____.

I don't_____.   I don't_____.

But I always_____.   But I always_____.

    And we both_____.

Language Arts

Global Carnival

Maybe I'll Just Stay Me!
A Poem for Choral Reading
by Karl A. Matz

I
I'd like to live in a grass hut,
that's the place to be!
I'd fish for my dinner every night
and swim in the deep blue sea.

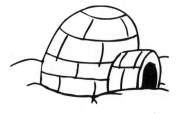

II
I'd like to live in an igloo,
that's the place to be!
Where the stars still shine at lunchtime
And snow is all you can see.

III
I'd like to live in a tepee,
that's the place to be!
I'd ride my pony as fast as the wind
On the prairie wide and free.

IV
I'd like to live in a houseboat,
that's the place to be!
I'd travel to all the oceans
And rivers and lakes
and seas.

ALL
I guess I'll live in the
home I have,
that's the place to be!
It's fun to pretend, to wish and to dream
but maybe I'll just stay me!

Global Carnival

If Only You'd Try
by Karl A. Matz

You could be
exactly like me
You can! I wouldn't lie!
You could have my skin,
my hair and my chin,
my cheeks and my toes,
my knees and my nose,
If only you'd give it a try.

Then get your friends to turn into me
and the world will be as the world should be.
With everyone walking and talking like me
and no one would ever be, ever be, ever be
lonely like me
anymore.

Global Carnival

NAME _____

Worksheet for "If Only You'd Try"

Directions:

After reading the poem "If Only You'd Try," get into pairs and complete the activities below.

1. Here is a list of some of the things the person in the poem wanted you to change about yourself. You and your partner can use it to find out how you are different and the same.

   _____   _____
             name   name

   SKIN   _____   _____

   HAIR   _____   _____

   EYES   _____   _____

   CHEEKS _____   _____

   TALK   _____   _____

   WALK   _____   _____

2. List some other ways people of the world are different.
   _____
   _____
   _____

3. Now list some ways people of the world are all the same.
   _____
   _____
   _____

© 1995 by The Center for Applied Research in Education

The Wise Milkmaid

A Play in One Act from a Folktale of Old Japan

Cast

    Narrator
    Oldest Sister
    Middle Sister
    Youngest Sister
    Merchant
    Mother
    Milkmaid

Setting: *The sitting room of a castle. As the play opens, the three sisters are tending to their tasks: cleaning, cooking, and laundry. The merchant sits in a fancy chair at upstage center.*

Narrator:	Long ago in Old Japan there lived three sisters. They worked for a cruel merchant who lived in a castle by the sea. The oldest sister cleaned the castle, the middle sister cooked the food and the youngest sister washed the merchant's clothing. After many months, they began to miss their mother. They went to their master and said,

(All three go to merchant and kneel at his feet.)

Oldest Sister:	Please let us go to visit our mother!
Middle Sister:	Yes. She is lonely and sick.
Youngest Sister:	We want to care for her and make her well.
Narrator:	The cruel merchant did not want them to leave. Who would clean his house, cook his food, or wash his clothing? *(Merchant shakes his head slowly. Sisters cry and plead silently.)* He said no again and again, but they cried harder. Finally he agreed.
Merchant:	You may visit your mother for two weeks. But you must each bring me a gift.
Middle Sister:	Oh, yes, kind master! Anything!
Narrator:	They agreed without thinking, for they were very happy at the thought of seeing their mother.
Merchant:	Oldest Sister, you will bring me fire in a cage of paper.
Oldest Sister:	But, Master, the fire will burn the paper cage and escape. How can I bring you such a gift?
Merchant:	Bring it or remain here with me. Middle Sister, you will bring me wind in a cage of wood.
Middle Sister:	But, Master, the wind will blow through the bars of the wooden cage and escape. How can I bring you such a gift?
Merchant:	Bring it or remain here with me. Youngest Sister, you will bring me a rainbow in a cage of glass.
Youngest Sister:	But, Master, the rainbow would shine through the walls of the glass cage and escape. How can I bring you such a gift?
Merchant:	Bring it or remain here with me.

Narrator:	The cruel merchant knew the three sisters could not bring him the gifts. He knew they would have to stay. But then the youngest sister said,
Youngest Sister:	Very well! We will bring you the gifts you want.
Merchant (*Angrily*):	Do not return without my gifts or you will be punished.

(Mother enters and sits in her peasant cottage. If possible a set or drop can be made to give the appearance of a cottage.)

Narrator:	*(As Narrator speaks, the three sisters cross to Mother. Mother greets the three daughters with smiles and hugs.)* The three sisters hurried down the road to the village where their mother lived. They were happy to see her and had a wonderful visit.

(Mother and sisters ad lib happy chatter as they prepare and eat a meal.)

Narrator:	Then the time came to return to their master. *(As Narrator speaks the sisters wave good-bye to their mother and cross to stage center. They stop and sit on the floor and begin to cry.)* As the sisters started their journey back to the merchant, they began to feel afraid. They had been so anxious to see their mother that they had promised gifts they could not bring. They knew their cruel master would punish them and they began to tremble with fear.
Oldest Sister:	What shall we do?
Middle Sister:	We cannot bring the gifts our master wants.
Youngest Sister:	We shall surely be punished.
Narrator:	Soon a beautiful maiden came down the road carrying her pails of milk.
Milkmaid:	Why are you crying?
Oldest Sister:	We have promised our master that we would bring him three gifts.
Middle Sister:	But the gifts he wants are impossible.
Youngest Sister:	We shall surely be punished.
Narrator:	They began to cry even more bitterly.
Milkmaid:	What gifts did your master ask for?
Oldest Sister:	I must bring fire in a cage of paper.

Middle Sister:	I must bring wind in a cage of wood.
Youngest Sister:	I must bring a rainbow in a cage of glass.
Narrator:	The milkmaid thought and thought and then she began to smile.
Milkmaid:	I know how to help you. Listen to me.
Narrator:	She whispered to the sisters and they began to smile, too.
Oldest Sister:	Thank you, wise milkmaid.
Narrator:	*(The three sisters skip across the stage to the merchant's castle.)* The three sisters laughed and sang as they skipped up the road to the merchant's castle. *(Sisters should pick up the lantern, the fan, and the crystal prism before arriving at the castle.)*
Merchant:	How dare you return to me without the gifts! Now you shall be punished.
Oldest Sister:	But, Master, we have the gifts. You asked me for fire in a cage of paper. Here is a paper lantern!
Middle Sister:	And you asked me for wind in a cage of wood. Here is a bamboo fan!
Youngest Sister:	And you asked me for a rainbow in a cage of glass. Here is a crystal prism!
Merchant:	You three are not clever enough to think of this. Who told you? Who told you?
Oldest Sister:	A wise milkmaid we met along the road.
Merchant:	Find her and bring her to me.
Narrator:	*(The sisters cross to stage center and sit down again.)* The three sisters left the castle and sat down on the roadside where they had seen the milkmaid before. *(Enter Milkmaid.)* Soon she came down the road carrying her milk pails. The three sisters took her to the castle to meet the cruel merchant. *(All four cross to the merchant's castle.)*
Merchant:	You are wise and beautiful. As a reward for your cleverness, I will make you my wife.
Milkmaid:	That is no reward. I do not want to be your wife.

Merchant:	WHAT? You are a poor milkmaid. How can you say no to me?
Milkmaid:	Put me in charge of your money instead. I will make you rich.
Merchant *(laughing)*:	No merchant has ever had a WOMAN in charge of his money.
Milkmaid:	Only those who are brave and wise grow to be rich. Are you brave enough to try it?
Narrator:	The merchant thought and thought.
Merchant *(to audience)*:	If I put her in charge of my money, the other merchants will laugh at me. But if she makes me rich, the laugh will be on them. Am I brave enough to try it? *(to Milkmaid)* Very well! Stay here, then. Be my manager and take over the affairs of my business. But if you do not make me rich, you will be punished.
Narrator:	The Milkmaid became the cruel merchant's manager and what do you think? She made him richer than his wildest dreams and made herself rich, too. *(The Merchant should sit alone while the three sisters look after the Milkmaid's every need—brushing her hair, polishing her nails, brushing her clothing, etc.)* The three sisters became the servants of the wise milkmaid. She was very kind to them and they served her well for many years.

The End

Global Carnival
Using the Play "The Wise Milkmaid"

1. **Produce the Play:** Students can learn the lines and present the play in a typical, on-stage performance.

2. **Readers' Theatre:** A small group of five may present it to the rest of the class as a "readers' theatre." The chief advantage to either form of presentation is the "deep-level reading" that takes place. The players read and re-read, learning new words and rehearsing them again and again until the new words become familiar, but they do so in the context of authentic experience, not just as a repetitive drill.

3. **Map the Story:** After the play has been presented, engage students in a discussion of the main themes of the story. As a large group, or in several small groups, they should be able to map the story as follows:

    a. **Setting:** A Merchant's castle in old Japan

    b. **Characters:** Merchant, three sisters, their mother, milkmaid

    c. **Problem 1:** Sisters want to visit their mother.

    Solution 1: They cry until he gives in.

    d. **Problem 2:** Sisters can't get the gifts.

    Solution 2: The clever milkmaid solves the problem.

4. **Seatwork:** Have the students compare and contrast this tale with others they know using the worksheet.

Global Carnival

NAME _____

Worksheet for "The Wise Milkmaid"

1. Which character in "The Wise Milkmaid" is good and kind?

   _____

2. Which character in "The Wise Milkmaid" is mean and cruel?

   _____

3. Think of another fairytale you know. List the character in that story who is mean and

   cruel._____

4. List the character in the other story who is kind and good.

   _____

5. What problems did this character have to solve? _____

   _____

   _____

6. How did this character solve the problems? _____

   _____

   _____

Language Arts

NAME _____

Write a Folktale!

Directions:

Use this story map to help you write a folktale.

1. List a **setting** for your folktale. _____

   _____

2. Choose a **kind and good character** for your folktale. _____

   _____

3. Choose a **mean and cruel character** for your folktale. _____

   _____

4. What is **one problem** your kind and good character needs to solve?

   _____

   _____

   _____

5. What is a reasonable **solution** to this problem? _____

   _____

   _____

   _____

© 1995 by The Center for Applied Research in Education

Language Arts

Global Carnival

Preserving Food
(a teacher-led activity)

Background:

Before scientists learned of ways to preserve foods, people had to do whatever they could to keep foods fresh. Italian, Mexican, and some Asian foods are spicy because people in those lands used to put heavy seasonings on meats that had spoiled to cover the taste. That's why the foods from those cultures are often very spicy and hot. Eskimo and Scandinavian foods are very bland because the natural climate is cold. Foods didn't have to be spiced because they could be frozen and kept fresh until needed.

Experiment:

What is the effect of heat and humidity on meat?

Materials:

Per Group:

3 tsps. raw hamburger

3 small bowls

A refrigerator

Salt

Procedure:

1. Place 1 teaspoon of raw hamburger in each bowl. Label one "No preservative," one "Salted," and the third "Refrigerated."

2. Place the "No Preservative" specimen out of the way in a safe, warm place.

3. Liberally salt the "Salted" specimen and place it near the first specimen bowl.

4. Place the "Refrigerated" specimen in a refrigerator.

5. After three days, observe the changes in the three specimens. Cut each lump in half and inspect the inside. What changes occurred in each? How do they differ? Is one more spoiled than the others?

Challenge:

Look on a map. Which countries would be the hottest and, therefore, have the greatest difficulty preserving food? Are these countries where the cultural foods are hot and spicy? What countries have foods that are not spicy?

Follow-up:

Have a traditional latino salsa with real tortilla pieces. Who likes it hot?

Global Carnival

Water Purification
(a teacher-led activity)

Background:
In some parts of the world clean drinking water is scarce. Some places have much sea water, but that is too salty to drink. In other places water becomes polluted by insects, plant growth, and the rotting of organic materials (dead animals, grass, and leaves). People all over the world have problems finding and storing drinkable water.

Experiment:
How can water be purified for drinking?

Materials:
Per Group:

Jug of distilled water

3 quart jars

3 small bowls

Measuring cup

Box of table salt

Soft cotton cloth or coffee filter

Saucepan

Sheet of glass or hard plastic

Spray bottle

Stove or hot plate

Procedure:

1. Measure equal amounts of distilled water into three quart jars.

2. Add enough salt to each jar to leave the water tasting salty.

3. Label the jars: "Filtered," "Aerated," and "Distilled."

Part 1: FILTERED WATER

Pour the salty water from the "Filtered" specimen through a filter into one of the bowls. Taste it. Did this filtering process remove the salt? Push one end of the cotton cloth into the jar of salty water and allow the other end to hang down into one of the dishes. After a few days the water will have been drawn through the cloth into the bowl. Taste the water in the bowl. Is it salty or "fresh"? Does filtering make salt water drinkable?

Part 2: AERATED WATER

Pour some salty water from the "Aerated" specimen into the spray bottle. Spray into a dish from a distance of about one foot until there is a sample sizable enough to taste. Is it salty or "fresh"? Is this process a good way to make water drinkable?

Part 3: DISTILLED WATER

Pour some water from the "Distilled" specimen into the saucepan. Heat to boiling. Catch the steam on the glass (hold it with a thickly gloved hand). Allow the drops to fall into a bowl until there is a sample sizable enough to taste. Does this process make the water drinkable?

Challenge:

In what parts of the world is fresh water most difficult to obtain? How do the people who live in these areas solve the problem of getting and storing fresh water?

Global Carnival

NAME _____

NAME _____

Measure Me!

Directions:

(1.) In pairs, measure each other. (2.) Compare by subtracting. (3.) As a class, find the records for greatest and smallest in each category. (4.) Find the averages for each category.

body part	name	name
1. head		
2. foot		
3. neck		
4. forearm		
5. index finger		
6. knee to floor		
7. spine to elbow		
8. height		
9. wrist		

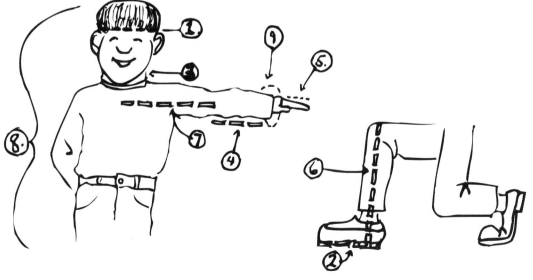

Global Carnival

NAME _____

Solve the Problems

Directions:
Use your arithmetic skills to solve the problems below.

Global Carnival

NAME_____

What's the Message?

Directions:

The problems below spell out a message. Use the code to figure it out. The answer to number 1 is the first letter, the answer to number 2 is the second letter, and so on. The first letter is done for you.

A	B	C	D	E	F	G	H	I	J	K	L	M	N	O	P	Q	R	S	T
4	10	14	15	20	21	24	27	30	32	35	36	40	42	45	48	50	54	56	60

U	V	W	X	Y	Z
63	64	72	81	100	120

1. $9 \times 8 = 72$
2. $10 \times 2 =$
3. $2 \times 2 =$
4. $6 \times 9 =$
5. $4 \times 5 =$
6. $4 \times 1 =$
7. $6 \times 6 =$
8. $9 \times 4 =$
9. $10 \times 6 =$
10. $3 \times 9 =$
11. $10 \times 2 =$
12. $8 \times 7 =$
13. $2 \times 2 =$
14. $8 \times 5 =$
15. $5 \times 4 =$
16. $9 \times 8 =$
17. $3 \times 9 =$
18. $2 \times 10 =$
19. $6 \times 7 =$
20. $10 \times 10 =$
21. $9 \times 5 =$
22. $9 \times 7 =$
23. $6 \times 10 =$
24. $7 \times 9 =$
25. $6 \times 9 =$
26. $6 \times 7 =$
27. $9 \times 5 =$
28. $9 \times 7 =$
29. $10 \times 6 =$
30. $6 \times 10 =$
31. $9 \times 3 =$
32. $4 \times 5 =$
33. $6 \times 6 =$
34. $6 \times 5 =$
35. $6 \times 4 =$
36. $9 \times 3 =$
37. $10 \times 6 =$

W __ __ __ __ __ __ __ __ __ __ __ __

__ __ __ __ __ __ __ __ __ __ __ __

__ __ __ __ __ . (Shel Silverstein)

Global Carnival

NAME_____

In Which Direction?

Directions:

Use a map or globe to answer these questions.

In which direction must you travel to get from:

Egypt to The Netherlands _____

South Africa to Australia _____

Rome to New York _____

Brazil to Hawaii _____

Japan to India _____

Germany to Chile_____

Nigeria to Chad _____

California to Alaska_____

Greenland to Greece _____

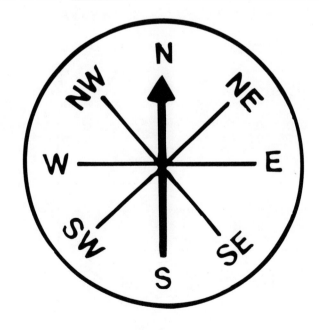

© 1995 by The Center for Applied Research in Education

Social Studies

Global Carnival

NAME _____

In Which Environment?

Directions:

Look at each job listed on the chart. What kind of environment would be needed? Name one country that has the proper environment for each job.

	coast	much land	lakes/rivers	long summers	country
fishing					
cattle					
shipping					
fruit farms					
tourism					
canning					
sea cruises					

Social Studies

Global Carnival

NAME _____

Where Should You Be?

Directions:
Where would you have to be to do each job listed below? Write that place on the blank.

1. Catch shrimp _____

2. Raise cattle _____

3. Be a lifeguard _____

4. Be a bull fighter _____

5. Raise llamas _____

6. Grow coffee beans _____

7. Study gorillas _____

8. Study penguins _____

9. Climb a mountain _____

10. Grow rice _____

© 1995 by The Center for Applied Research in Education

Global Carnival

OJO DE DIOS,
Spanish for EYE OF GOD
(a teacher-led activity)

Materials:

Two 8" x 1/4" dowels or craft sticks per child (If you're adventurous, the Native Peoples who originated the artform used raw sticks from trees)
Two skeins of variegated yarn

Procedure:

1. Use yarn to secure the two sticks into a cross. Start with the end of the yarn and wrap diagonally first one way then the other until the sticks are immobile. (See Figure 1.)

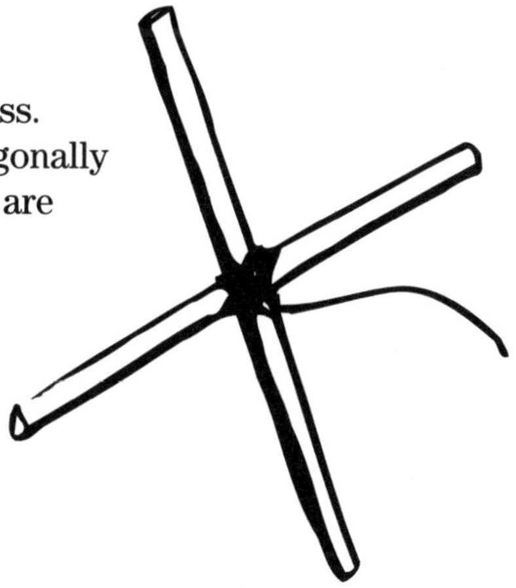

Figure 1

2. Begin weaving the yarn around the stick. Pull the strand across the front of the stick, then loop it around the stick, then proceed to the next stick in a clockwise fashion. When one complete trip around the frame has been accomplished, the next strand should be laid beside, but never crossing the previous strand. (See Figure 2.)

Figure 2

3. At the weaver's discretion, the yarn strand can be cut and another color tied on. This should not be done too often, however, because the knots where the two colors are joined become noticeable. Three or four color changes give a nice pattern to the finished work. (See Figure 3.)

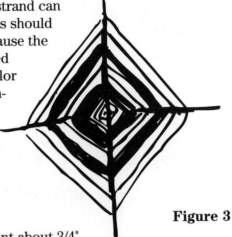

Figure 3

4. When the weaving has reached a point about 3/4" from the end of the sticks, the strand should be securely tied down and snipped off. (See Figure 4.)

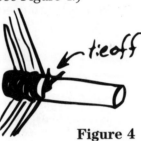

Figure 4

5. Attach tassels to the two side sticks and the bottom stick. (See Figure 5.) Then the OJO DE DIOS can be hung in the classroom to give a rich, multicultural flavor to the room. (See Figure 6.)

Figure 5 **Figure 6**